ECOTONES

Investigating Sounds and Territories

AF597636

EDITED BY VALENTIN BANSAC, MIKE FRITSCH, ALICE LOUMEAU & PETER SZENDY

ECOTONES
Investigating Sounds and Territories

SPECTOR BOOKS

Prelude

Valentin Bansac, Mike Fritsch, Alice Loumeau & Peter Szendy

The Luxembourg Pavilion at the 19th Architecture Biennale in Venice is an invitation to close our eyes and actively listen. The installation hosted in the pavilion, *Sonic Investigations*, operates a radical shift away from the visual: it offers a cartography of various environments exclusively through sound. The present volume, conceived as a companion to the sound installation in Venice, has a broad ambition: it argues for a counterproject to the hegemony of images.

Since the climate crisis can also be understood as a crisis of sensory perception and representation, it is all the more urgent to find new ways of approaching the ongoing environmental transformations. The act of listening allows for different forays into both anthropic and natural ecosystems. It directs our attention toward the vocality of other-than-human agencies; it empowers them with a voice of their own.

Field recording can thus be the prelude to another mapping of the world, attuning our ears to its various fault lines, to its tensions. And *sounding* becomes a powerful investigative tool, a way of auscultating the infrastructures of the present as well as the times to come. The concept of *ecotone*, a transitional space between two ecosystems, is a guiding thread for the authors of this volume as they listen to boundaries between territories, to urban patterns, to natural balances and imbalances, or to political fractures.

*

Our collective investigation crosses the borders between various disciplines—art, architecture, philosophy, social sciences, infrastructure studies, anthropology, etc.—and zigzags through multiple forms or genres: theory, fiction, poem, visual essay, case study ... David George Haskell considers listening as a moral act of resistance, whereby embodied sonic memories are passed on. Madelynne Cornish and

Philip Samartzis, from the Bogong Centre for Sound Culture, use their diverse array of microphones to record climatic alterations in the Australian high plains. Xabi Molia's short story walks us through the resonant ruins of abandoned cities. Peter Szendy explores the potentialities of the concept of ecotone for an auscultation of the climate to come. Emma McCormick Goodhart senses underwater auditory practices, from fish listeners to bioacoustic monitoring technologies.

In a visual essay and an email conversation, Valentin Bansac, Mike Fritsch, Alice Loumeau, Peter Szendy, and Ludwig Berger document their approach to mapping the sonic elements of shifting ecotones where Luxembourg's natural landscapes and digital economy meet. Shannon Mattern considers listening as a methodology for engaging with and intervening within urban infrastructures and logistics.

Environmental sounds and structural resonances are blended in Nadine Schütz's installation for an industrial bridge in the city of Saint-Denis. Laura Vazquez and Cole Swensen capture the poetic echoes of light and sound. Together with a collective of artists and researchers, Laure Brayer gathers sonic evidence and aural testimonies on the transformation of the Romanche valley in the French Alps. Soline Nivet and Ariane Wilson follow the lead of eerie sounds from a blind Parisian façade and unearth cables connected to the global communications network. Julia Grillmayr, Christina Gruber, and Sophia Rut, from Lobau Listening Comprehensions, take us through their sonic chronicles of the Danube wetlands. Yuri Tuma, co-founder of the Institute for Postnatural Studies, imagines a Silent Academy as a place for healing in the dystopic aftermath of Sonic Wars. Tim Ingold objects to the concept of soundscape.

ECOTONES

Investigating Sounds and Territories

Memory, Ecology, and Sound

David George Haskell

Birdsong awoke in me one of my earliest memories. The remembrance was buried so deep inside that I was not aware that it existed until I heard the Eurasian blackbird sing. The bird's melody dislodged the memory, helped by the evocative timbre of the sound. The bird sang from a perch on a rooftop, on the edge of a large courtyard inside a block of apartments in Paris, France. The tall buildings created a reverberant space in which the song gained a glow, an extra richness imparted by the space into which the bird threw its gorgeous voice. No other bird sang, and the only other sound was the low-pitched rumble of the city.

I was nearly fifty years old when I heard the blackbird sing and the memory was reawakened. At the time, I was renting a small apartment for a few days to visit family in Paris. I expected nothing more than a convenient place in which to stay, but what I experienced was a sensory portal into my childhood. The experience was beyond language at first. On hearing the song, I felt transported into the apartment my family had lived in when I was three years old, an apartment that also looked out on one side to an open courtyard. This translocation and feeling of deep familiarity with the song started as pure feeling, then expanded and caused me to ask questions. Why was the bird giving me a strong sense of belonging and familiarity? Did blackbirds sing in the courtyard behind our building when I was an infant? I telephoned my mother, and she confirmed, "Oh, yes. Every spring a blackbird sang. It liked to perch on a potted shrub that someone had put out on a high balcony."

My mother also told me that, for her, the song sounded sad and alone. She grew up in the countryside, surrounded by birdsong of many kinds. The solitary voice of the blackbird sounded to her like an impoverished springtime, one missing many of its voices. But I had no such experience of blackbirds elsewhere. For me, this was the only birdsong of spring. I do not remember how I reacted at the time, but the song's beauty must have caught my attention because it wormed its way into my neurons and lay, sleeping, for nearly fifty years. During those decades I lived mostly in the United States and never in a place where Eurasian blackbirds sang behind my home in the spring. When I rented temporary accommodations in Paris all those years later, I was suddenly in a place where sonic memory and the sensory experience of the moment converged. In an instant, the dormant memory sprang to life. This sound was a time traveler contained within my body, yet I was unaware of its existence until the moment that I heard the song.

To remember sound is a form of personal sonic archaeology. We excavate from our memories the embodied knowledge that each of us carries in the connections between neurons in our brains. It is in these connections that memory resides. This knowledge is often highly specific to place. It was not just the up-and-down notes and trills of the blackbird's song that were part of my memory but the way the song behaved within the courtyard, bouncing repeatedly from wall to wall, creating a golden reverberation that gave the song a special richness. Yet, our culture offers us few opportunities to spend time with these experiences of sonic memory, to celebrate them with others, or to query what they mean in an era of rapid change.

The ability to remember sounds over many decades is a particularly human quality. Compared to our close mammalian cousins—the great apes and the monkeys—human sonic memory is remarkably well developed. Nonhuman primates have an excellent memory for visual and tactile experiences, but these powers do not extend to sound, especially in the long term. Species more distantly related to humans such as whales and songbirds sometimes have good long-term sonic memories, remembering details of songs for months, sometimes years. But these, too, are exceptional among animals. For most animals, hearing is a forgetful sense.

For we humans, our excellent sonic memory surely evolved to help us with language. Our linguistic prowess relies on a good sonic memory. We remember for decades not only the meaning of particular words, but what subtle inflections and changes of emphasis mean within a sentence, revealing to us the emotional textures of language. We also remember the unique timbre and pacing of the voices of people we know well. If you were to hear a recording of a loved one who died many years ago, you would instantly know their voice.

At a neurological level, this excellent sonic memory in humans seems to come not from the enlargement of one specific part of the brain but from better interconnections within it as a whole. Compared to other species, we have especially well-developed links between the parts of our brain used for the perception and comprehension of sound, links that are much weaker in other primates. Scans of human brains show that these nerve pathways are required for long-term sonic memory. If sounds have a special emotional resonance for us, we are more likely to remember them. After all, we forget most of the trivial details of what we hear each day, even those sounds that we pay attention to in the moment. If I ask exactly what words the shopkeeper spoke to you last week or which birds were singing on the city street on a particular day in June, you would likely not remember. But most of us remember well the distinctive sounds of our childhood homes, the textures of the speech of loved ones, and sounds that emerge at times of heightened emotion, such as beautiful experiences of live music or horrific times of war.

Although our excellent long-term memory first evolved to help us with human language, this memory also gives us an ecological compass. People who move from one continent to another often experience homesickness for the birdsong of their former homes. The same is true for the hubbub of city life, which, if we grew up amid its liveliness, feels soothing even though it can be loud. Aural memory, then, allows us to understand and navigate both the human and more-than-human worlds. We carry within us an internal geography of sound. Our memory helps us to access this embodied spatial knowledge.

The remembrance of individual sounds (like birdsong) and of the feel of soundscapes (the overall sound of a forest or a city, for example) gives us points of reference through which to assess and understand our world. These sonic memory maps vary across space, but they can also change through time. When voices are lost or new sources of sound emerge, we understand through our senses that the world is changing. This sensory memory then complements intellectual reflection on the nature of a changing world and adds intuitive emotional texture to these thoughts.

Recently, the power of sonic memory to understand change has had technological help and enhancement. Around the world people are deploying digital recording devices that use tiny microphones and circuit boards to "hear" and store all the sounds within the devices' frequency range. Sometimes, this range approximately matches that of the human ear. But some devices also extend to higher frequencies, such as the ultrasonic microphones that record bat and insect calls and song. Others expand the range lower, into what we humans call infrasound, to detect the low-frequency calls of some ocean-dwelling whales and of forest elephants or the low tones of waves crashing on a beach. All this sonic "data" is captured and held in digital form, a type of extended memory that is so vast in terms of the amount of data it holds that no human will ever listen to even a fraction of what we have gathered. Instead, we turn to algorithms to "listen to" and interpret the world. As we should expect from any technological extension of human capabilities, these new methods reveal many insights but also carry with them inherent problems or dangers.

The insights are especially useful in projects that aim to use sound to understand the diversity of life in threatened habitats. By recording forests, meadows, coral reefs, seagrass meadows, and cities, then feeding the stored memories of the sounds of these places into algorithms, we can gain an overview of changes to the diversity of sound-making organisms in these habitats. Until the advent of these technologies, such a comprehensive approach to the changes in entire soundscapes would have been impossible. To sift through recordings using human ears to document every insect voice, anthropogenic sound, and other sound in one location for months would take decades of study. Now, answers pop out of the algorithms with much greater speed. We can, for example, offer rapid assessments of the vitality of forests, understanding how logging or other changes to the forest alter the combined voice of all the singing or calling animals in the region.

At a time of biodiversity loss, stored sonic data can serve as another measurement of what the living Earth is losing under our sometimes-improvident care. More usefully than simply documenting loss, the data can also inform management decisions, telling us, for example, where to focus conversation efforts or allowing us to use the types of forest management that least impact biodiversity. In this way, digital memory of the recent past—lodged inside computer chips—can help us to build a future that is more life-filled and sustainable than would otherwise have been possible. It is on this hope that much bio- and eco-acoustic monitoring is now focused.

Less directly, but perhaps just as important, the vast troves of new sound recordings from around the world offer people an opportunity to listen to and thus understand the state of the world's ecologies. Most of us have no direct sensory connection to the habitats where our food, timber, and consumer goods come from. This is disastrous for human ethics. With no sensory connection to the consequences of our actions, there is no possibility for embodied understanding. As sensory animals, to be cut off from such stimulus is to be adrift, with no mooring to the materiality and ecology of the world except through disembodied intellect and emotion. This seems a perilous position for any species. Given the extraordinary power of our species, the peril extends to the vitality of the whole living Earth. Those artists, activists, and scientists who are sharing recorded sounds with the general public are therefore engaged in work of profound ethical significance. In reconnecting our human senses to the voices of the Earth, they put our bodies back into right relationship with the larger community. Sharing recorded fragments of sonic memory is one way to encourage and enable listening as a moral act. Listening, then, is not a passive activity but an active reconnection of the state of the "outside" world and the direction of the "interior" world of ethical discernment.

In addition to the many opportunities they offer today, sound recordings also create an archive for the future, digital memories of the sounds of contemporary Earth. People in future decades will listen to these recordings with questions we cannot imagine. Every stored recording is a gift to tomorrow. We pass on sonic memory, encoded in tiny electrical digital charges.

There are three dangers in this new form of sonic memory. The first is that the technologies draw human effort and attention away from the world as it is, the world manifest in our vibrant human senses, and instead direct it ever deeper into the world of electronics. We spend more time staring at the laptop than listening to the world. The name of these new technologies—passive acoustic monitoring—hints at this problem. "Passive," rather than active. Can one more technology that requires us to spend our days and nights plugged into algorithms change how we collectively treat the Earth?

The second danger is that new technologies will further marginalize the very people with the most lived human experience of endangered habitats. In tropical forests, for example, local communities have hundreds or thousands of years of accumulated cultural experience of listening to the forest. Their livelihoods depend on the forest's integrity. Yet, both commercial and conservation activities sometimes displace these people from their lands. The biodiversity crisis is also, sometimes, a human rights crisis. Western scientists have had a tendency to fly in, deploy their technologies, then fly back out to publish and sometimes implement their "solutions" to forest loss. If technological forms of sonic memory follow these unjust practices, they are unlikely to contribute to positive futures. Fortunately, many scientists and nonprofits are now aware of this problem and are using the technologies to empower rather than circumvent local communities.

The third problem is that the digital memory of habitats could be used as a form of greenwashing. The algorithms that interpret digital memory can be set up to yield misleading conclusions. For example, finding a loud and diverse soundscape in a logged forest could be misused by unscrupulous or ignorant land managers to claim carbon or biodiversity credits. The fact that the interpretation of recorded sonic data is so statistically complex and ambiguous makes this a very real risk. Scientists have told me that such greenwashing is already being marketed. Distorted sonic memory of this kind could undermine the goal of biodiversity protection.

All these problems are an extension of the unsettling revolution started by the very first sound recordings back in the nineteenth century. Until then, all sound was of the moment, an ephemeral experience that could be remembered but never exactly recreated. Then, using traces on smoked glass and waxed cylinders, humans figured out how to capture and store what had been fleeting. Imagine the dislocation felt by those who first heard their recorded voices. No human had ever had this experience before. Until that time, we heard our own voices only through the convergence of bone conduction and transmission through the air, which bring the vibrations to our inner ear and then, through nervous signals, to consciousness. With recorded sound, we could suddenly hear ourselves as others hear us. The same was true of instrumental musicians. They could now hear a "replay" of their performances. Music went from being a precious experience of the present, stored in human memory and in the imperfect sketches of musical scores, to something that could be called up from recorded memory many times.

Today, we live saturated in recorded sound, and so we forget what a revolutionary transgression of time and memory was created by the first sound recordings. Now that we have "outsourced" so much sonic memory to recording devices outside of our bodies, do we devalue the memories carried within us? Further, recorded sound is fed to us by "streaming" companies that measure our engagement with every podcast or song. Our listening to recorded sound is thus often quantified and commodified. Strangely, listening in the moment and using embodied sonic memory—the use of our ears and brains unaided by other technologies—has become an act of resistance to algorithms that seek to extract "data" and profit from us.

Memories of sound are not just carried in brains and electronics. Words and stories also carry sonic memory. Every written word carries sound inside it. Especially in alphabetic languages, inked marks on the pages symbolize sounds, as do the marks in musical notation. So, every stroke of a pen is a crystallization of sonic experience, a memory carried on the page. When we read words or music, these sounds are activated within our minds, letting us hear the voice or music of the writer, awakening the dormant memory carried in the symbols on the page. Each letter or note is a micro-memory of sound.

In addition, the meanings of the words that we read carry with them memories of sound. When we read descriptions of sound, we reinhabit the author's experience. There is a double layer of memory at work here. First, the author remembers sound as they write the description.

The written word thus emerges from the layers of bias and selective attention that every listener brings to sound. Then we readers create a second reawakening of memory as we engage with the words on the page and hear the sounds come to life in our imagination.

In my own work as a writer, I use many literary techniques to conjure sonic memories from the past and bring them to life for readers. I try to animate the memory of sound so that, when read, the words leap into vivid remembered experience. For example, in *The Songs of Trees*, I use an underwater microphone to share with readers the experience of hearing snapping shrimp. The sound is a strange one, outside the usual range of everyday experience, and so I enliven and energize the memory of this sound using several methods, here briefly labeled in a quotation from the book: "When I first release the hydrophone, all I hear is the high gurgle [onomatopoeia, as the g's evoke the sound] of streaming water. As it descends, the swirling sounds fall away. Suddenly I'm plunged into a pan of sizzling bacon fat [a metaphor, using an analogy to an everyday sound as an imaginative bridge into the memory of the sound]. Sparkles surround me, a sonic shimmer [repeated use of s's to bring the sound to mind for readers]. Every glistening fragment is a fleck of sunlit copper, warm and flashing [synesthesia, as I experience both light and a sense of heat as I listen]. I've arrived in the acoustic domain of snapping shrimp." Writing, then, serves the purpose of breathing life into sonic memory, so the memory can be activated inside the conscious experience of others.

Not all stories are written, of course. The stories we hear from our loved ones are often the most emotionally powerful memories of sounds. Oral storytelling is therefore a portal into past sounds. I vividly remember my grandfather telling me about the sounds of birdsong from his youth in the 1930s in northern England. He lived in a rural area, and the hedgerows, fields, and forest fragments were fat with the sound of birds, especially in the spring and summer.

When I was a child and he was an old man, in the 1970s, he told me, "Those sounds are now nearly all gone. The countryside is nothing like it was. It seems empty to me." The sadness he felt as he related this to me was very evident. Because we were close, I felt the sadness, too. And the memory of birdsong from the 1930s jumped from him to me. Although I was not born until decades later, he transferred a fragment of memory to me. The sounds of those birds—and then the absence of those sounds—became, through his story, part of my own sonic memory and understanding.

In the years since my grandfather told me this story, I have read, as a biologist, hundreds of technical papers about bird populations. But none stick in my memory in the same way that his story does. Why? Because the story came to me from someone whom I loved and it arrived as a spoken tale, not an abstract graph or written analysis.

Today, the challenge for all of us is to create these memories to share with others. We must listen in the present moment so that we can have stories to tell in the future. Our children, students, friends, and neighbors will need to hear from us what the world sounded like today. This will form part of their own memory and sonic compass in a changing world.

Sound seems so ephemeral and insubstantial. It seems to leave no obvious trace of its passage. But this is an illusion. Sonic memories persist within and around us. Excavating and honoring these memories can teach us about the knowledge we carried embodied within, a form of knowing that networks us to the voices of the living Earth. In this way, memory and ecology—literally, "the study of home"—are interwoven.

I stated earlier that our culture offers few opportunities to find and explore experiences of sonic memory, but this is not entirely accurate. In some realms, especially in communal experiences of music, we gather together to listen, explicitly for the purpose of interweaving present sensory experience with sonic memory. Can we now expand these practices into the more-than-human world? Perhaps gather with friends to toast the return of birdsong in the spring? Or point out to family members how every tree sounds different in the wind? From these seemingly minute and unimportant impressions we accumulate an extraordinary gift, embodied memory of the living Earth.

The Bogong High Plains Sound Map

Madelynne Cornish & Philip Samartzis
(Bogong Centre for Sound Culture)

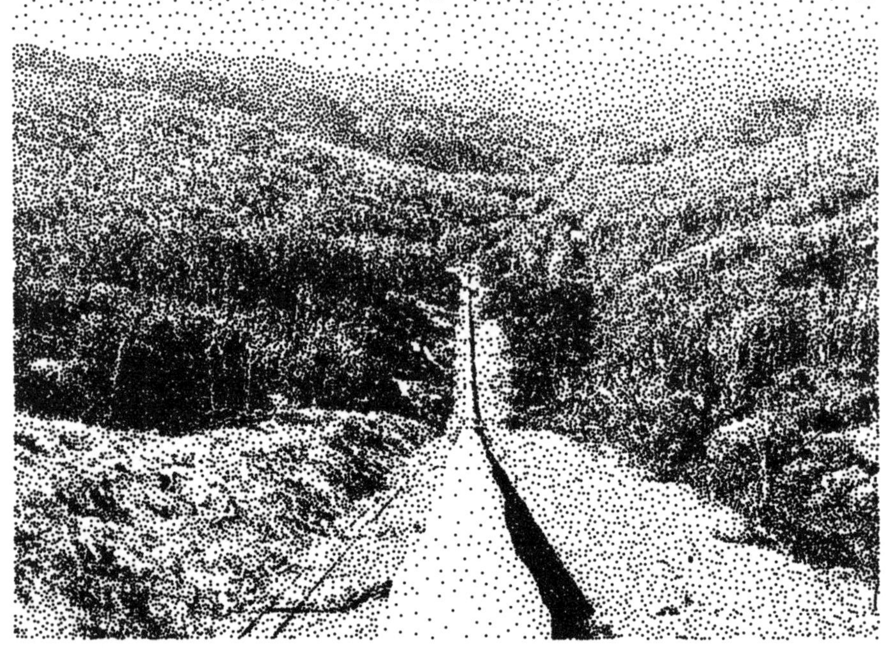

Kiewa Valley, Philip Samartzis

INTRODUCTION

The Bogong Centre for Sound Culture (B-CSC) is an artist-led initiative dedicated to exploring the relationship between sound, art, and the environment. Through residencies, workshops, and public programs, the B-CSC fosters artistic practices that engage deeply with the natural world, particularly the unique ecosystems comprising the Australian Alps. Its work bridges contemporary sonic art and ecological awareness, encouraging audiences and artists alike to consider the ways in which sound reflects and influences the understanding of place, memory, and ecological change.

THE PLACE

The Bogong High Plains, located 350 kilometers northeast of Melbourne, are part of the Great Dividing Range, a vast system of mountains, plateaus, and hills stretching along Australia's east coast. In winter, this area becomes one of the largest snow-covered regions in the country. The landscape consists of heathlands in sheltered areas and grasslands in windier, exposed zones. Rich, organic soils are found in wetlands, where water lingers for at least a month each year. Rare snowpatch herbfields appear in places where snow lasts well into the summer. Scattered throughout the plains are snow gums, a hardy eucalyptus species able to survive extreme cold. The area was heavily damaged by the 2003 Eastern Victorian alpine bushfires, which were sparked by lightning strikes. The fires merged into one of the largest and longest in Victoria's history, burning over a million hectares in two months.

The Bogong High Plains have deep cultural significance for the Bidawal, Dhudhuroa, Gunaikurnai, and Nindi-Ngudjam Ngarigu Monero peoples, who traditionally traveled to the area during summer. They gathered to feast on Bogong moths—a vital seasonal food—and take part in ceremonies and meetings. Since European settlement, the most significant changes to the landscape have come from agriculture, grazing, and the Kiewa Hydroelectric Scheme. Built in the 1930s, the scheme captures mountain streams through a network of aqueducts, dams, and tunnels. These streams feed into catchments, including Pretty Valley Pondage and Rocky Valley Dam, powering a sequence of hydro stations that generate electricity.

At an elevation of 1,800 meters, Falls Creek Alpine Resort acts as a gateway to the plains. It includes lodges, chalets, and apartments, mostly built from the 1980s onwards, designed with materials and colors that blend into the environment. The resort is surrounded by snow-gum woodlands, alpine bogs, and streams. Birds like the crimson rosella, flame robin, and Australian raven are common here. Outside of winter, a heavy silence settles over the area, occasionally broken by the sounds of snowmelt, creaking structures, and distant birdcalls.

One striking feature of the region is the ghostly remains of trees left after the fires. Their gray, hollow trunks stand as stark reminders of the destruction. When the wind moves through the dead canopy, it creates a soft, mournful sound, contrasting with the rustle of new growth sprouting from their roots.

The ever-present sound of water—whether flowing, dripping, or pooling—adds to the character of the landscape, while streams, creeks, and billabongs shaped by natural processes and human infrastructure, such as aqueducts and pipes, channel water into turbines for power generation.

The region's climate is harsh, with wind, moisture, and cold constantly battering the landscape. Human-made structures—including communication towers, barriers, and signage—groan and shudder under the pressure, adding an industrial undercurrent to the natural chorus. These combined elements form a restless, multilayered soundscape that reveals both the beauty and the precariousness of the Bogong High Plains.

Winter transforms the region into a hub for recreational tourism, with up to ten thousand visitors a day during ski season. The sounds of vehicles on snow chains, skiers with clattering gear, chair lifts, snow machines, and grooming vehicles dominate the landscape. Regular medical evacuations, shrill music, a general hubbub, and the constant hum of infrastructure add further complexity to this busy winter soundscape.

THE MAP

The Bogong High Plains Sound Map is a collection of field recordings capturing the unique sounds of the Bogong High Plains and Kiewa Valley. It explores how climate change, industrialization, environmental stress, and tourism impact this fragile alpine ecosystem. The website uses real-time weather data to activate sound recordings that match current atmospheric conditions, creating a dynamic and interactive way to experience the archive. This connection to live data makes the sound map an evolving representation of place, emphasizing the influence of changing weather, seasons, and human activity on the environment.

Unlike traditional maps, which rely on visual elements such as boundaries, elevations, and landmarks, sound maps focus on acoustic features that bring places to life through their unique auditory signatures. By capturing natural sounds like rushing streams, gusting wind, and birdsong alongside industrial sounds—such as those produced by hydroelectric systems, ski infrastructure, and tourism—sound maps reveal the subtle and often-overlooked ways in which landscapes are shaped and transformed. Seasonal shifts are also documented, from the muffled silence of snow-covered plains in winter to the buzzing of insects and trickling of melting snow in summer, offering a fuller spatiotemporal understanding of the environment.

The recordings, collected over two years, showcase how the alpine environment responds to both natural processes and human intervention. They provide an auditory record of key environmental changes, including the lasting impact of bushfires, the constant hum of water-management systems, and the disruptive noise of seasonal tourism. Sound maps serve as both art and documentation, combining field recordings with photographs and written descriptions to highlight environmental, cultural, and topographic features within the landscape. They create multisensory experiences that invite listeners to engage with place in new ways, encouraging deeper reflections on its past, present, and future.

A diverse selection of microphones was employed during fieldwork to register subtle yet profound indicators of climate change. Condenser microphones, sensitive to high-frequency sounds, were strategically placed to record the calls of birds, frogs, and insects. These sounds provide critical insights into changes in biodiversity, such as shifts in migratory bird patterns and altered insect activity caused by rising temperatures. Ambisonic microphones were deployed near waterways to monitor the sounds of flowing streams, recording changes in water flow and volume that reflect the melting of snow and reduced precipitation patterns. Ambisonic microphones capture sound in full 360-degree spatial detail and are useful in registering the intensity and direction of water flow and complex environmental characteristics, deepening our understanding of hydrological changes and nuanced ecosystem dynamics. Hydrophones, submerged underwater, recorded the acoustics of alpine streams and lakes, and the effects of freezing and melting during winter and spring. To capture the volatility of extreme weather events, such as thunderstorms, blizzards, and severe wind gusts, omnidirectional microphones were used to convey dynamic and visceral representations of atmospheric change.

Accelerometers were employed to measure structural vibrations in dams, turbines, and pipelines as a means to record how weather and climate influence the behavior of hydroelectric infrastructure. These solid vibration sensors detected subtle shifts in movement resulting from fluctuating water levels, extreme weather events, and temperature changes. Variations in rainfall and snowmelt, for instance, alter water flow and pressure, affecting vibration frequency and amplitude. Similarly, temperature fluctuations cause materials to expand or contract, influencing structural stability. Accelerometers provide valuable insights into how climate-driven factors impact the resilience and performance of hydroelectric systems and the attendant infrastructure.

The Bogong High Plains Sound Map plays an important role in fostering environmental awareness and advocacy. By amplifying the soundscapes of vulnerable ecosystems, it draws attention to the impacts of climate change and human activity that may not be visible to the eye. In this way, it acts as both a form of creative expression and a scientific tool, preserving the acoustic heritage of a location and offering insight into its ecological health. For places like the Bogong High Plains and Kiewa Valley, where delicate balance and competing forces define the landscape, the sound map weaves together the voices of the natural and built environments, creating a layered narrative that reflects the ongoing relationship between humans and nature. It invites audiences to actively listen, encouraging a sense of connection, curiosity, and responsibility toward these fragile spaces.

By reimagining the way places are mapped and understood, sound maps challenge conventional methods of storytelling and cartography. They offer an accessible and immersive way for audiences to engage with remote areas that are often hard to reach, capturing fleeting and ephemeral sounds that embody the character of a place. Through the integration of real-time data, recordings, and environmental shifts, the Bogong High Plains Sound Map becomes both a historical archive and a living, breathing reflection of a unique and ever-changing cold-climate ecology.

CONCLUSION

Through its innovative approach to art and ecology, the B-CSC invites audiences to imagine new possibilities for how we might understand our planet. It asks us to listen—not just to the sounds of place but to the stories they tell and the futures they call on us to create. In a world increasingly defined by disconnection and division, this is a philosophy that resonates far beyond the Australian Alps, offering a profound reminder of the power of art to bridge the gaps between us and the world we share. Sound artists play an increasingly vital role in observing and recording the tension between climate, landscape, technology and human action, to reveal the intricate connections that bind them together.

The Last Song of the Cities

Xabi Molia, translated by Cole Swensen

We spent three days near the first abandoned city, Saint-Étienne. The installation of the microphones took an hour or two, and each sound recording lasted exactly fifteen minutes. My master told me to close my eyes during the recordings, but I didn't always, and sometimes I secretly watched him listening, his eyes closed, his face gray and scowling. I often wondered if we were hearing the same thing through our headphones, or if our backgrounds, our memories, and our desires sculpted the composite mass of sounds coming toward us in different ways.

In hindsight, I must add that from our first mission on, I felt certain that my master heard *farther* than I, that his hearing probed the depths of space, as if he was searching for something, perhaps an anomaly or a certain kind of presence.

The master had insisted that I never talk about what we heard. Words, he said, could never get close to truly describing sound. Words were like curses; once named—*vibration, growl, warbling*—sounds lost their quality of uncertainty, which the master said I should consider one of their fundamental characteristics. "Sounds are always indecisive," he declared.

Perhaps because I didn't name them, I remember nothing of the sounds of Saint-Étienne.

During the next expedition, we listened to the ruins of Turin. In a history class, I'd seen an Italian film shot in the mid-twentieth century, and they all spoke rapidly and profusely. Though we couldn't really know, we presumed that Italians were a people more lively and boisterous than most. I dreaded hearing, in the very fact of the city's silence, the depressing proof of their disappearance. But to tell the truth, the Turin that I heard was neither more nor less funereal than the other abandoned cities.

I wasn't the only initiate that went along on that expedition; a young woman named Lucia came with us. During some of the recordings I saw that she, too, kept her eyes open. When our glances met behind the master's back, we smiled at each other.

Later, she broke the second rule. We were walking up the ramp leading to the roof of an immense parking structure where our module had landed, with the master trailing far behind us, when Lucia asked me in a low voice what I had thought of the birdsong. When I heard the word *song*, a jolt shot through me. I knew perfectly well which recording Lucia was referring to: two hours earlier, in an ecotone, we had set up our microphones not far from a great, eternal machine, and after several minutes, invisible birds, who must have gone silent or flown off when we arrived, began singing. It was rare. It was beautiful. I whispered to Lucia, "It was beautiful." And I added, without really knowing what I meant, "You'd have said it was a song of gratitude."

Lucia didn't come along on the following expeditions. But I retained, as if she'd passed it on to me, the urge to take notes in a journal that I kept secretly in my cabin. In it, I listed the objects and, more rarely, the beings that I'd recognized during the recordings. I described the sounds in a few words, mostly nouns, with an adjective thrown in here and there. And finally, growing bolder, I began to write down the impressions that these soundscapes evoked for me.

Later, I learned that the General Command was disappointed with our work. My master's superiors were not impressed by his methods. The numbered recordings that he sent them gave neither date nor location. Our sonic material was thought too crude, and its scientific value too meager. Are there lost ones still living in the ruins? There was no evidence of it in our recordings.

Summoned, the master repeated what he'd told me at Saint-Étienne about words. And, according to the official record, he added that the particular locations where the recordings had been made were not important for this project. Quite the opposite: "Hypotheses regarding their integration into imaginary geographies will likely create an undesirable interference with the more generic points I wish to present." He was asked to reconsider his position.

As we left, he told me to take notes after every recording. When I asked him what he wanted me to write down, he shrugged his shoulders and said, "Like in your notebooks. What you imagine you're hearing." I didn't pursue this allusion to an activity I'd thought was secret. So my written reports would be sent in along with our recordings. The master made it clear that he would never read them.

The next stretch of work was, for me, the happiest. After each recording, I carefully detailed all the impressions it had evoked in me. It made me feel like I was doing something publicly useful each time I noted the sonic differences among the abandoned cities, among the ways that they made silence. A collection began to accumulate. Listening to them, some cities sounded cold, others warm. I heard Warsaw as furious, and the howling of wolves rose from the empty center of Barcelona, the city that seemed to me to be the most menacing of all those we sounded, a city sharply on the lookout. From the remains of Lisbon, creaking noises erupted at regular intervals, seeming sometimes to answer, sometimes to complement each other. I wrote: "Lisbon: like a troubled conversation."

My reports clearly didn't please them either; the master, impassive, told me that they'd been judged "too personal." He added, "Command doesn't think there could possibly be any wolves in Barcelona." And then he confirmed what I'd feared—that the funding for the program would be cut at the end of the year. Considering preparation, travel, and the quarantines, we'd only have time to sound two more cities.

He let me choose the penultimate one; I opted for San Sebastián, where my parents had been born. The master must have known this, but said nothing.

We listened to the city for two days. The sea was rough, and its loud (I wrote “gray”) roar filled several of our recordings. It was the sea that my parents must have heard, and the sound had no doubt remained the same, unaltered. I tasted the pleasure that I’d come looking for that of sharing something, deferred but identical, with beings that I’d barely known. I mentioned this to my master. At his slight frown I thought he was going to object, but he remained silent, I think in order not to mar my joy.

For the last city, the master chose Glasgow. He said that he chose it at random, but I didn’t believe that. The last city, marking the end of our whole project—who could give that over to the indifferent hands of chance? Sensing my doubts, the master remarked that what we had documented on the devastated continent was the sound of all cities, of any city—a disaster, he said, was measured by its degree of monotony

I no longer know whether to believe in his theories. Did he only advance them to silence his opponents? To mask an obsession that he thought was probably forbidden?

He was lying about Glasgow. I learned from a colleague that a woman he had loved had died there, or at least it was presumed so, as she had been living there when the catastrophe struck.

We took longer than usual to install our microphones. The fine drizzle slowed us down, as did a pervasive sadness. During these last two days, I kept my eyes open to watch the master listen. And through my headphones, I listened to him listening. Several times on the second day, his eyes gleamed and his face stiffened. I so hoped a song would rise from the ruins, that a woman’s voice would call from the distance No such thing reached my ears, but will I ever know what the master heard that day?

As we were about to take off again, he turned to me and said goodbye. He wanted to stay, he said, to "verify" a few things. I asked if he would like to keep any or all of our equipment, and he said no, that I would need it. Then he headed off toward the city, his silhouette disappearing between two misty buildings; I never saw him again.

I thought of going back to base, but then I deactivated my tracer and set out for San Sebastián. I burned the module and also disappeared.

Every day, I record the city. I hear nothing and I hear everything. I hear everything that remains and everything that came after. Sometimes I feel that I know the city better than it knows itself. It seemed to me that by listening to it, I became a part of it. I am a part of it, and I even believe that it needs me. If I stopped, no doubt the new murmurs and songs that I hear from time to time, the muffled detonations, the nocturnal harmonies—the entire imaginary life of the city—would disappear with me.

Ecotonalities

Peter Szendy, translated by Simon Horn

At the threshold of the twentieth century, a word lodges in the English language for the first time. It settles there to fashion its abode, its realm, its zone. And from there this linguistic species, at first endemic to English, will migrate toward other languages, French, in particular. Attentive observers of lexical environments have tracked its emergence to a study published in 1904 by the American botanist Frederic Clements.[1]

The new word—I will have it wait for a moment (it has, after all, waited centuries and centuries to come to light)—emerges in a paragraph dedicated to the "zonation" of plant habitats. These are, as it turns out, laid out as a function of favorable thermal and hygrometrical conditions about a point that constitutes a center (a pond, a lake, for example) or along an axis of symmetry (a river, a waterway). It is to designate the border between one mode of vegetal population and another that the botanist forges, before our eyes, this neologism: *ecotone.* Such will be the unheard-of technical term for the "stress line" delimiting diverse ways of occupying soil, regimes of habitation. Immediately one reads, between parentheses, the etymology of this lexical creation: *oikos* means habitat in Greek (the house, the home); and *tonos*, the result of tensing, of stretching with force, as of a string.

The word is the subject of an entry in the glossary of the systematic treatise that Frederic Clements published the following year, *Research Methods in Ecology*, where it is defined as "the tension line between two zones." And it regularly returns to inhabit his later writings: in 1916, in *Plant Succession*, it is synonymous with "transition area" or "transition zone," sometimes playing the role of "a record of the effects of small variations of climate"; meanwhile the monumental *Bio-Ecology* of 1939, cowritten with the American zoologist Victor Shelford, introduces the notion of "ecotone species"—namely, "rhythmic migrants" among organisms, passing from one zone to the other in a cyclical manner, like certain crabs whose habitat changes with the cycle of high and low tides.[2]

Having once emerged within the field or yield of the English botanical lexicon, the concept of ecotone migrated toward other horizons. Not only transplanted into other languages, it also began to flower in other ecosystems of thought. In 1981, the authors of an article on the prehistoric landscapes of England hypothesized that the circular megalithic structures at certain sites could represent "demarcation symbols standing in a cultural 'ecotone,'" which is to say that they would signal the limit between inhabited enclave and open expanse.[3] The inverted commas flanking the word ("'ecotone'"), like standing stones marking its linguistic enclave, indicate a case of recent transplantation, a migration whose strange effect is still being felt. These marks of alterity that surround and circumscribe the term tend thereafter to disappear, as is the case in a recent work which hypothesizes that "ecological and cultural ecotones may intersect: ecotones such as seashores and deltas can be ... life zones where human communities interact."[4] Is this to say that the neologism emerging in 1904 in the study of the American botanist thereafter acclimated not only to other linguistic spheres but also to other domains of thought? Has "ecotone"—the word—become a cosmopolitan lexical species? Such questions echo those posed by Jacques Derrida in one of his rare (too rare) texts that abut ecology, notably when he asks himself: "What would an ecosystem be for discourses?" Or, again, when Derrida himself bows his ear to a term that is "a recent artefact," the result of "a modern and unstable graft of Greek and Latin": "Is this synthetic object, the word 'biodegradable,' biodegradable?" To wit: can it vanish, "let itself be assimilated, circulating anonymously within the great organic body of culture," there to implant itself all the better since it would be somewhat forgotten in its dissolution?[5] Questions analogous to those posed by the brief history of the word "ecotone," as I have just sketched it in rough outlines: this word, once it is no longer a limitrophe lexical event between several linguistic zones or discursive fields, this word, which itself had something ecotonal in its manner of suspended abode upon taut lines of partition, is it now put up everywhere as if in the comfort of its own home? In a word: has it *relaxed* in its generalized usage?

To exhume, as I have, its supposed point of origin and to map the way it radiates from its lexical source will have the merit, I hope, of restoring to it that tension that gave it birth. Of letting it be heard, pricking our ear to the *tonos* vibrating therein. For, as will be clear, it is *tone* that draws me here, as a new category for listening to, for auscultating, ecosystems in their becoming.

A METEOROLOGICAL HARP

Moving back before the lexical invention of Frederic Clements, let us begin to plot—program for linguistic excavations to come—the traces of the surfacing of a *tonal*, namely tensile, paradigm in relation to milieu, to environment, to climate. I dig up first this, buried among the strata that media archaeology is attempting to bring to light: a singular instrument, christened *armonica meteorologica*, that its inventor, the Italian Jesuit Giulio Cesare Gattoni, canon of the cathedral of Como, describes in a letter published in 1785.[6]

It is "a new type of gigantic harp," he writes, made of fifteen metallic strings stretched between, on one side, "a tower 52 braces high" (the Italian brace being, at the time, a unit of measure a little longer than half a meter) and, on the other, the fourth floor of a house situated "150 paces distant." Contrary to what its name might suggest, the *armonica* in question had therefore nothing to do with the glass harmonica devised by Benjamin Franklin in 1761, for which Mozart composed a quintet. It sooner resembles a "large-scale Aeolian harp," as E. T. A. Hoffmann remarks in the fantastical tale of *Tomcat Murr*.[7]

Before he puts it to service in his meteorological experiments, Gattoni yields to the musical charm of his giant instrument: "I assure you, sir," he declares to the addressee of his letter, "that it was in those first days truly diverting to run through the different strings plucking them [*tasteggiandole*] as on a harp, and to feel this strange and new-formed instrument respond to the fingers in most delicate concert." To play thus upon the *armonica meteorologica* defers its true usage a little. Only a little, since Gattoni quickly stops his musicking: "Quickly I perceived that the pleasure could not endure," he recalls, as if he now had to hurry to compensate his pleasant procrastination.[8]

And indeed, we will see, it will also be a question of delay and anticipation when the megaharp, by virtue of the tonal tension of its strings, its more or less taut tuning, becomes an instrument for sounding the not-yet- and soon-to-come weather. It is this properly meteorological usage that Gattoni describes, with extreme minuteness, under the rubric of a list of "data" and of "facts." Let us read the first of them: "Fact 1. On August 20, 1784, after some time of calm and peaceable skies the vibrations of the armonica began to be felt [*sentire*] at various reprises, every two or three hours, then more frequently during six days together. . . . On the 27th came the rain, which for three days continuously inundated the town with very rare intervals of reprieve."[9] These vibrational intimations, Gattoni explains, relate primarily to the sense of touch: "Before the sound begins to be heard, if one applies the pads of the fingers [*i polpastrelli delle dita*] to the string, one feels a light beating . . . which resembles the pulsing of animal arteries; then the vibrations gradually increase, and make themselves more frequent, as in the heat of fever." Vibrational tactility thereby precedes sonority, which, for Gattoni, seems to be the intensification of its forerunner.

Yet perhaps one should sooner say that string tension is a limitrophe phenomenon, which ceaselessly oscillates (vibrates, indeed) between the tactile and the tonal. If one considers the zones of the sensible that it puts in play, namely the haptic and the sonic, as two aesthetic ecosystems—one would need to say *aesthesic*, the better to mark that they relate to sensation, to Greek *aisthēsis*, and not to art or beauty—then vibration is ecotonal, in the sense that it occurs at the limit, on the endlessly recrossed boundary between touching and hearing. It is, moreover, this ecotonality of the vibrating string that is translated, in the account of "Fact 1," by Gattoni's use of the Italian verb *sentire*, which means just as much to feel as to hear ("the vibrations of the *armonica* began to be heard [*sentire*] at various reprises"). In moving to the second of the "facts" he enumerates, *sentire* clearly gives place, however, to *udire*, to hear: "Fact 2. In the current year 1785 the first three days of February were calm, and the sun shone splendidly: that notwithstanding, the strings were heard at various times of day, and by night, to sweetly rumble."[10]

Gattoni relates that among those whom he summoned to bear witness to his experiments, the physicist Alessandro Volta, inventor of the electric or "voltaic" battery, was skeptical as to the predictive power of what really must be considered a veritable *proacousia*, a listening bent toward what promises to be. But Gattoni vindicates the exactitude of his meteorological prophecies: the strings, he insists, stretched between a tower and a house just as they are stretched between two regions of the sensible, detect by their *tensile tonality* the vanguard signs of the coming weather. It is their stress line, to take up the expression of Frederic Clements, that shows itself premonitory in announcing the weather that has not yet come yet is already here. A weather, a time—a *temps*—that should hereafter be called heterochronic, since it does not coincide with itself: it touches tensed strings even before it manifests itself in the shape of rain or snow; it precipitates in advance of itself before ever forming this or that precipitation.

BIOTREMOLOGY AND AUSCULTATION

If Gattoni were an animal, he would doubtless be a spider (despite his name which, in Italian, inevitably evokes a large cat). For it is the spider that, thanks to the strings or cables that compose its web, can feel, can catch, distant events. Its woven work constitutes, as the arachnologist and neurobiologist Friedrich Barth writes, “a self-made extension of its sensory space,” an aesthesic expansion that transmits vibrations from one network point to another.[11] Just as Gattoni laid his finger on a metallic string, quivering from the effect of atmospheric variations, and felt or heard the coming tempest weaving its plot in the distance, just so the spider, lurking somewhere in its net, lets the last phalange (the tarsus) of one of its legs trail on a string of its silken *armonica*, so as to be alerted in the event of a tremor. Differences of amplitude among the signals that circulate on this vast exteriorized perceptual apparatus will, in turn, permit the spider to precisely locate the prey caught in its snare. Biotremology, the study of vibratory communication in living organisms, has shown that certain predators that feed on spiders know how to move across a web in a way that minimizes the shuddering that would reveal their presence: they develop what has been called a “vibrocrypsis,” which is to say, a camouflage proper to a haptic world.[12]

Spiders are not content to passively await the moment in which they will receive notice of some change in their reticulated environment. In order to detect the presence within the web of dead insects or stuck detritus, they also conduct active soundings: with their forelegs they shake the web’s radial filaments and use the information borne by the vibration’s returning echo to place the obstacle that it encountered. Here is a tactile equivalent of what, for example, bats or dolphins do when they emit sonic signals, whose repercussions detail the form and content of their surround.

It was the American zoologist Donald Griffin who, in 1944, proposed the name *echolocation* for this perceptive technique, consisting in “locating obstacles by means of echoes,” emitting sounds that will be reflected, like rebounding arachnid vibrations.[13] In the article where he introduces this neologism, he insists on the intonation that must be adopted in pronouncing it: “It seems best to accent the first syllable in order to make clear that the word echo is employed," he writes, as if he were folding the new name back on itself, doing to the term what the term designates—to wit, locating the echo.

Just as the word *ecotone* vibrates, doubtless still relatively strangely, in the reticulated linguistic space where it resides (it has not completely biodegraded in the midst of language, we could say with Jacques Derrida), so too the term *echolocation* continues to shake the network of language along each of the paradigms in which it resonates. At the crossing of these paradigmatic filaments, it is easy to mistake oneself and hear another neologism forming by interference: *echotone*. Is this the result of a simple phenomenon of accidentally crossed wires, or is there some necessity to its formation? Let us make the following hypothesis: if an ecotone is a stress line, a *tonos* between two *oikoi*, the echotone could be the sonic symptom of a difference in tension, the phonic expression of a discord, a distension within an apparently uniform body or milieu.

The medical practice of percussion, later supplanted by that of auscultation, is surely the perceptual exercise that, on the human scale, best corresponds to an echotonal symptomatology. One could in all likelihood find many animal equivalents, as Jules Michelet imagined when, conflating auscultation and percussion, he described the behavior of the woodpecker: "At first the skilful forester, full of tact and experience, tests his tree with his hammer—I mean his beak. He listens, as the tree resounds, to what it has to say, to what there is within it. The process of auscultation, but recently adopted in medicine, has been the woodpecker's leading act for some thousands of years. He interrogates, sounds, detects by his ear the cavernous voids which the substance of the tree presents."[14] True, scientific studies of the woodpecker have shown that its hammering is not properly auscultatory, that it is more a communication related to territory or mating, a phonation whose acquisition is similar to that of birdsong.[15] All the same, the idea that percussion and auscultation are nothing especially human is largely confirmed by the perceptive techniques deployed by other species, like the echolocalizing bats or vibroceptive spiders that we have met in the conceptual web that is attempting to weave itself here.

The stethoscope devised by the French doctor René-Théophile-Hyacinthe Laënnec for what he qualified as "mediate" auscultation—whose execution he codified in his treatise of 1819, many times revised with various additions[16]—was, by the middle of the nineteenth century, sufficiently widespread to be the object of satirical texts warning against its abuse, while preserving the stamp of its relative novelty. In 1848, Oliver Wendell Holmes, who continued in Paris the medical studies he had begun in Boston, composed a poem entitled "The Stethoscope Song." It follows the misadventures of a young practitioner who, having bought "a stethoscope nice and new," fails to notice what, unbeknownst to him, spins itself within: "It happened a spider within did crawl, / And spun him a web of ample size, / Wherein there chanced one day to fall / A couple of very imprudent flies."[17] One of the flies was large, the other small and thin: "So there was a concert between the two, / Like an octave flute and a tavern gong." Even in an obvious case of fictional caricature, it is striking to note that this critique of the infatuation with auscultation introduces an arachnoid dimension. But above all, the resonant universe that thereby opens (in which one hears, borrowed from the lexicon of Laënnec and quoted in French in the poem, a *bruit de râpe* or *râle sifflant*—a rasping noise, a whistling rattle), this whole rustling world that the stethoscope reveals, is produced by the play of difference between two sonorities, namely the high- or low-pitched buzzing of two trapped insects. Like the percussion whose heritage it claims, auscultation—as we see—is a listening to difference.

PERCUSSION AND ORGANOGRAPHY

In its revised edition of 1828, Laënnec's treatise is crossed, striated, by numerous vibrating strings. It might be a haptic sense that first detects their vibration, as in the case of a "*frémissement cataire*" (a light shuddering caused by the narrowing of a cardiac valve and similar to the purring of a cat—*cattus* in late Latin) or in the case of a pulmonary catarrh: "When the resonant bass rattle has its seat in a branch close to the surface of the lung, if one applies the hand to the corresponding point of the wall of the chest, one often feels a shuddering analogous to that given by a taut vibrating string."[18] But each time, audition rapidly takes over from touch, and hence the analogies that come to characterize the resonances registered by the cylinder of the stethoscope are musical: "The resonant bass rattle," one reads a few lines further on, "is strong enough to imitate the sound of a prolonged bow-stroke upon the fat string of a cello."[19] Elsewhere, "the noise of the vascular murmur" is described as "a whistling analogous to that of the wind which passes through a keyhole or the resonance of a metallic string that vibrates long after it is touched."[20] It is all as though the vast textual corpus with which Laënnec attempts to register bodily noises were itself reticulated after the fashion of a spider's web, woven in filaments, or of a meteorological megaharp of metallic cables.

And indeed, in this aesthesic network where tactile and audile ceaselessly alternate on the ecotonal limit that separates them, the vibrations are perceived and analyzed in an essentially differential way. The ear and the touch of the auscultating-percussing doctor are essentially *comparative*: "When *comparatively percussing* the two sides of the chest," writes Laënnec, "one must take care to percuss the two kindred points successively, strike them with an equal force and at exactly the same angle."[21] Likewise, to determine that a coughing, spitting patient presents "a rather marked bronchophonic resonance about the tip of the left shoulder blade", it is necessary to place the stethoscope in many places on the body in order to locate, differentially, the source of the sonic symptom.[22] Percussion and auscultation therefore produce a true phonocartography, as can be heard in reading the report on the examination of a carter suffering from emphysema and suffocating catarrh: "The thorax gave a very clear sound across its whole extent, except the right posterior and interior, where it was almost nothing. The breathing, explored by the cylinder, was hardly perceptible and mixed with a bit of rattle, now mucous, now hissing, along the whole extent of the left side of the chest."[23]

Auscultation extended the practice of percussion theorized half a century prior by the Austrian doctor Joseph Leopold Auenbrugger: "It . . . widens its usage to many diseases in which percussion alone tells nothing," Laënnec writes in the first edition of his treatise.[24] Reciprocally, it is in seeking to enrich the older percussive practice via Laënnec's new auscultatory technique that Pierre-Adolphe Piorry develops the idea of a mediate percussion that, akin to a stethoscope, is accomplished by the intermediary of an instrument called a pleximeter, a kind of amplifier of vibrations that can be made from various materials (its inventor preferred ivory, but others made do with wood, or copper, or even the left index finger placed on the body and tapped by one or two fingers of the right hand). In the work that was to systematically reveal the advantages of the invention, one may read the following analogy: "The sound that the percussed pleximeter gives corresponds exactly to the part of the cavity being percussed. This fact is easy to establish: inflate your cheek with air and apply the instrument, now on the maxillary bone and now on the buccal wall, and alternately percuss these two points, and you will have a very different sound across two variant regions. The same test can be done wherever a bone is contiguous with soft parts."[25] Thereby, Piorry was able to propose a veritable technique of organ cartography, an *organographic* procedure, which he describes, for instance, in the report on his labors in support of his candidacy for the Academy of Sciences: "For since each organ has a structure and consistency proper to it, since each gives sounds and tactile sensations particular to it, it results that, at each point on the skin corresponding to the line of demarcation of that organ, it suffices to make a mark with the pencil to neatly indicate this line. ... It is after this fashion that mediate percussion becomes one of the principal means of organographism."[26]

Many in number are those today who, like Piorry, attempt to map afflicted or weakened bodies by registering their vibrations. This vibratory or sonic organography—thus, this tremorganography, phonorganography—is practiced not only on the vegetable or animal organism but also on what Hegel already called "the geological organism," that is to say, "the Earth-body," of which he even considers the "limbs."[27] Like the canon Gattoni almost two and a half centuries ago, those who are recording the geo-organism's vibrations lend their ear to the advance heralds of climatic changes. The scale is nevertheless not the same: it is not a question of a village or city but of the planet. And what is at stake are no longer simple variations of not-yet- or soon-to-come weather, but the anticipation of an inexorable point of no return that threatens, in the coming decades, to tip the world into the uninhabitable.

GLACIAL PHONATIONS

Touch and hearing, in the reticulated extension of their aesthesic ecotone, are accordingly expanded when outfitted not with vibrating strings stretched between tower and house, but with microphones. Hydrophones, for example, collect the soundwaves generated in oceanic waters by the wanderings of icebergs detached from the pack. And the glaciologists who auscultate these great unmoored blocks monitor the long-term portents of rising waters and disrupted major marine currents, regulators of global temperatures.

As with the spiders described by Friedrich Barth, here, too, listening alternates between an active practice and a passive reception: the first consists in emitting sonic impulses and deducing by the return of their echo the form and location of the obstacles they have struck (the principle of sonar, analogous to the echolocation practiced by dolphins or bats); the second consists simply in detecting the "sounds of life and death" of an iceberg, without introducing artificial signals into the ocean, without contributing to its phonic pollution with test sounds.[28] This latter listening—call it noninvasive—reveals, as to the sonic biography of the monumental being of ice that is the iceberg, essentially two types of phonation. The one: long vibrations at the extreme low register of the audible (a sort of basso profundo, even an infrasound) accompanied by a spectrum of harmonics resulting from the scraping of icebergs one against the other or on the sea floor. The other: brief signals closer to white noise, constituting so many phonic expressions of the fractures caused by melting, preludes to the breaking-up and ultimate disappearance of the iceberg. Such is the "voice" of the wandering glaciers, such are their vocal inflections.[29]

Their propagation in the aquatic milieu can be heard at distances measured in the thousands of kilometers (harmonic vibrations produced near the Antarctic peninsula can be detected at the equator), mixed with animal sonorities like the calls of marine mammals, with the noise of breaking waves, the patter of rain, the anthropic noise pollution of maritime transports, even the explosive reports linked to extractivism (techniques for the acoustic sounding of ocean deeps notably employ air cannons). In this vast confluence of the geophonies, biophonies, and anthropophonies of the world, glacial phonations are the expression of a differential of forces, which is to say, of a *tonos*:[30] the audible manifestation of a resistance, a discord, a tearing and fissuring, should the tension grow too strong. It creaks, it scrapes, it gnashes, it groans—it rattles, it sibilates, to borrow the lexicon of Laënnec—because a mass of ice forces its passage against the elevations of the sea floor, like the air that traverses bronchial secretions and there causes bubbles to pop.[31] The vast geological limb that the iceberg constitutes (detached from the shelf by what is called *calving*, as if a calf of ice had just been born) grates against another part of the terrestrial organism and, in this grating, it distends and contracts, it separates from itself in an expansion that stretches it despite the recalcitrant cohesion that maintains it. Glaciological tensivities are tonal because they are tonic (*tonikos*, in Greek, is said of what stretches or can stretch itself, but also of things relative to intonation and accentuation).

And it is there that the auscultatory paradigm imposes itself, essentially consisting as it does in distinguishing and situating the sounds of a body, small or large, afflicted by hollows, by intervals, by gaps. Whether in a micro-, meso-, or macroorganism, even unto those geocorporal masses, blocks of ice adrift, or the meteoric formations announcing variations in atmospheric pressure, what the auscultator seeks—human, arachnid, even machinic, equipped with tightened strings, with a tarsus, or a hydrophone—is the distensional and contensional tension of a being that recedes from itself and nears itself, in vibration, in resonance.

In a certain way, every resonating body is an ecotone, a stress line, between itself and itself. Every body, qua body held together by a certain tonicity, becomes ecotonal in the vibratory elasticity that pushes it to disjoin from itself, all while restraining it close to itself. It becomes the rhythmic migrant, so Frederic Clements would say, of its ipseity: it does not cease from crossing and recrossing, one way, now another, the frontiers that delimit it.[32] But reciprocally, the vibratory or sonic mode that seizes a body is always a symptom of inner discords that striate and run it through, as-yet-imperceptible faults that already riddle it, fractures and ruptures weaving their plot.

Percussion and auscultation sound for fissures in becoming, more as their endophony than their endoscopy. On our geo-organism, crossed today by stress lines unheard of—distended to the point of rupture along ecotones vibrating harder than ever—percussion and auscultation register in advance, by proacousia, the weather—the time—that has not yet quite come about, within the heterochrony that announces it in advance.

NOTES

1 Frederic E. Clements, "The Development and Structure of Vegetation," *Botanical Survey of Nebraska*, vol. 7 (The Botanical Seminar of the University of Nebraska, 1904), 153.

2 Cited in succession: Frederic E. Clements, *Research Methods in Ecology* (The University Publishing Company, 1905), 316; Frederic E. Clements, *Plant Succession: An Analysis of the Development of Vegetation* (The Carnegie Institution of Washington, 1916), 75, 416, and 109; Frederic E. Clements and Victor E. Shelford, *Bio-Ecology* (John Wiley & Sons, 1939), 326.

3 Robin Holgate and Paul Smith, "Landscape Studies in Prehistory: Two Examples from Western Britain," *Bulletin of the Institute of Archaeology* 18 (1981): 186.

4 Markus Arnold, Corinne Duboin, and Judith Misrahi-Barak, introduction to *Borders and Ecotones in the Indian Ocean: Cultural and Literary Perspectives* (Presses universitaires de la Méditerranée, 2020), 14.

5 Jacques Derrida, "Biodegradables: Seven Diary Fragments," *Critical Inquiry* 15, no. 4 (1989): 828 and 815–16.

6 Sig. Ab. Don Giulio Cesare Gattoni to Don Pietro Moscati, letter, September 16, 1785, in *Opuscoli scelti sulle scienze e sulle arti*, ed. Carlo Amoretti and Francesco Soave, vol. 8 (Milan, 1785), 298. This strange *armonica*, the existence of which seems to have aroused hardly any interest, except anecdotally, would surely merit a place in the *variantology* that Siegfried Zielinski proposes—namely, an "anarchaeology" opposed to a history of media founded on the idea of their progress. Siegfried Zielinski, *Deep Time of the Media: Toward an Archaeology of Hearing and Seeing by Technical Means*, trans. Gloria Custance (MIT Press, 2006), 7.

7 E. T. A. Hoffmann, *The Life and Opinions of the Tomcat Murr*, trans. Anthea Bell (Penguin, 1999), 125.

8 Amoretti and Soave, *Opuscoli*, 300.

9 Amoretti and Soave, *Opuscoli*, 300–301.

10 Amoretti and Soave, *Opuscoli*, 301.

11 Friedrich Barth, "The Vibrational Sense of Spiders," in *Comparative Hearing: Insects*, ed. Ronald Hoy et al. (Springer, 1998), 230.

12 Beth Mortimer, "Biotremology: Do Physical Constraints Limit the Propagation of Vibrational Information?," *Animal Behaviour* 130 (2017): 170.

13 Donald Griffin, "Echolocation by Blind Men, Bats and Radar," *Science* 100, no. 2609 (1944): 589. Friedrich Barth speaks of "a kind of *vibratory echolocation*" among the spiders he studies: Barth, "Vibrational Sense of Spiders," 230.

14 Jules Michelet, *The Bird,* trans. W. H. Davenport Adams, (London, 1869), 227–28.

15 Eric Schuppe et al., "Forebrain Nuclei Linked to Woodpecker Territorial Drum Displays Mirror Those That Enable Vocal Learning in Songbirds," *PLOS Biology* 20, no. 9 (2022).

16 René-Théophile-Hyacinthe Laënnec, *De l'auscultation médiate ou Traité du diagnostic des maladies des poumons et du cœur* (Paris, 1819).

17 Oliver Wendell Holmes, "The Stethoscope Song: A Professional Ballad" (1848), in *The Complete Poetical Works of Oliver Wendell Holmes* (London, 1895), 60.

18 René-Théophile-Hyacinthe Laënnec, *Traité de l'auscultation médiate et des maladies des poumons et du cœur*, new ed. (Brussels, 1828), 66, 479 ("L'application de la main . . . n'est réellement utile que dans un cas particulier, celui de l'existence du frémissement cataire"), and 508.

19 Laënnec, *Traité*, 67.

20 Laënnec, *Traité*, 497.

21 Laënnec, *Traité*, 15 (my emphasis).

22 Laënnec, *Traité*, 102.

23 Laënnec, *Traité*, 144.

24 Laënnec, *Traité*, 13; Auenbrugger's Latin work *Inventum novum ex percussione thoracis humani ut signo abstrusos interni pectoris morbos detegendi* was translated into French by Jean-Nicolas Corvisart in 1808, under the title *Nouvelle méthode pour reconnaître les maladies internes de la poitrine par la percussion de cette cavité*, published as an appendix to the *Essai sur les maladies et les lésions organiques du cœur et des gros vaisseaux* (Paris, 1855). On the history of percussion and auscultation, see my essay, *Of Stigmatology: Punctuation as Experience* (Fordham University Press, 2018), 44ff.

25 Pierre-Adolphe Piorry, *De la percussion médiate et des signes obtenus à l'aide de ce nouveau moyen d'exploration, dans les maladies des organes thoraciques et abdominaux* (Paris, 1828), 26.

26 Pierre-Adolphe Piorry, *Exposé analytique des principaux travaux d'anatomie, de physiologie, d'hygiène, de chirurgie, de médecine pratique et de littérature philosophique de P.-A. Piorry* (Paris, 1856), 18.

27 Hegel, *Philosophy of Nature*, §§ 337, 338, and 339, trans. A. V. Miller (Clarendon Press, 2004), 273, 277, and 278 [modified by translator]. If the aforesaid geological body or organism is admittedly "the dead product," if its limbs are "soulless," the Earth, Hegel insists (*Zusatz* to § 339, p. 335), is nonetheless "preserved by all these conditions which constitute a single chain, one whole."

28 Robert P. Dziak et al., "Life and Death Sounds of Iceberg A53a," *Oceanography* 26, no. 2 (2013): 10–12. On the distinction between "active acoustics" and "passive acoustics" (one also encounters the expression "passive listening"), see, in particular, Grant B. Deane et al., "The Underwater Sounds of Glaciers," *Acoustics Today* 15, no. 4 (2019): 14.

29 It was the geographer and militant anarchist Élisée Reclus who—in his *The History of a Mountain*, trans. Bertha Ness and John Lillie (New York, 1881), 127—spoke of how "the heat of the sun has endowed with voice and motion" the hitherto-silent glacier. Olivier Remaud insists on this glaciological "vocality" in his *Thinking Like an Iceberg*, trans. Stephen Muecke (Polity Press, 2022), 82.

30 It was Bernie Krause who proposed this tripartite terminology (geophony, biophony, anthropophony); see, for example, *Voices of the Wild* (Yale University Press, 2015), 11–12.

31 On the "*râle sibilant*," see Laënnec, *Traité de l'auscultation médiate*, 48–49; when the whistling is "muted and very light," Laënnec speaks of "subsibilant respiration" (ibid., 74). The bubbles formed in encumbered respiratory passages are the object of innumerable phonic descriptions, compared now to the "roll of a drum" or the "sound of a carriage rolling on paving stones" (ibid., 43), now to the "soft noise of a valve" (ibid., 67).

32 This is at root what Hegel says in the paragraph of his *Philosophy of Nature* (§ 300) consecrated to sound as "trembling": namely, that it is simultaneously "the momentary negation of parts" (the vibrating body divides from itself, negates its cohesion) and "the equally momentary negation of their negation" (the division closes and the parts aggregate anew, the body maintains itself). Hegel, *Philosophy of Nature*, 137 [modified]. I have closely auscultated this passage in *Of Stigmatology*, 65ff.

Censation in Substrata

Emma McCormick Goodhart

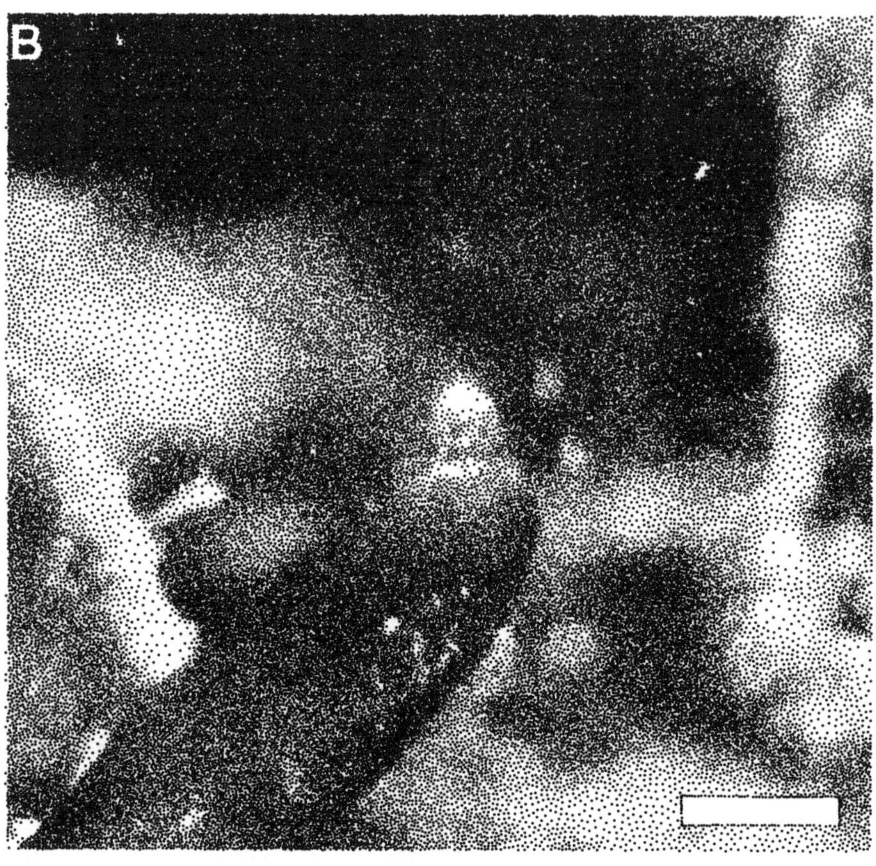

From Simon E. Freeman et al., "Photosynthesis by Marine Algae Produces Sound, Contributing to the Daytime Soundscape on Coral Reefs," *PLoS ONE* 13, no. 10 (2018): e0201766.

The sea is a natural laboratory
for altered sense ratios.[1]

You are not censors but sensors,
not aesthetes but kinaesthetes.[2]

If a world fashions organs of listening
adapted to its encoding, how can organs
participate in the receding of a world as
a movement of organic inadaptation . . . ?
Can one listen from the unencoded
conditions of an otherworld?[3]

I encounter the US Defense Advanced Research Projects Agency (DARPA)'s Persistent Aquatic Living Sensors (PALS) program (2018–23) just after I learn of ecopoetic practices of fish listening, used in lieu of sonar, in Southeast Asia, where fisherpersons submerge themselves underwater, as if free diving, to determine the motions (and even species) of schools of fish solely via bone conduction.[4] Amphibious, ancestral, unaugmented, and embodied, such divinatory listenings produce and perform biosonar in liquid "depth tech" and mirror those myriad, vibrotactile modalities through which marine organisms themselves register and emit sound in undersea environments.

Planetary wetworlds are ready-made acoustic channels, finely tuned for long-distance transmission across pressurized subdimensional thicknesses, for sound propagates over four times faster in water than in air. It also bends. Here, sound moves through and maps what sight can't. Listening by mediatic proxy, always beyond "anthroposonic" thresholds of audibility, becomes our aptest spatial prosthesis for imaging ocean space, itself dubbed by bio-, geo-, and anthropophonic strata in perpetual remix.[5] Even seafloor rock types can be identified by acoustic extension.

DARPA funds high-stakes, frontier technology development among academic, corporate, and governmental partners in deep science and other fields—part of a larger national security mission to deter war. Under DARPA's Biological Technologies Office umbrella, PALS's multidisciplinary research initiative is (strangely) not dissimilar in premise to that of fish listening and reads to me as soft science fiction, piquing my interest in how it proposes to outsource the task of sense-making subaquatic "territory" to wetware-led assemblages rather than hardware arrays; to intercept already networked intelligences of marine lifeforms in situ, making clear the extent to which biosensors, as experts in *umwelt*, still outperform their synthetic substitutes, including active sonar.

By tapping instead into marine organisms' "exquisite sensing capabilities"—"ubiquitous, self-replicating, self-sustaining"—the scheme seeks to architect "long-endurance, widespread sensory coverage" so as to strategically enable "overall maritime situational awareness."[6] Within PALS's tri-phase framework, teams of scientists from a handful of institutions (alongside requisite softwares for signal processing) record, analyze, and attempt to decode the nuanced, multimodal reactions of communities of marine organisms—whether sonic, behavioral, chemical (via lunar cycle–induced bioluminescence), tactile, or other—in order to indirectly detect the presence of either manned (MUV) or unmanned (UUV) undersea vehicles, ultimately alerting a remote end user to it.[7]

One monitors biology, not the target, in this configuration.[8] First circulated in 2018, the program's transscalar prompt urges prospective scientific teams to "consider organisms from bacteria to macro-organisms as well as multi-organism interactions," pushing conceivable sensing-agent communities well beyond antecedent cross-species collaborations. Often with "celebrity vertebrates," the US Navy's Marine Mammal Program, operative since 1959, trains bottlenose dolphins and California sea lions in "choice captivity" to detect and recover potential underwater threats.[9] (Selected PALS case studies included benthic soundscapes, black sea bass, Goliath grouper, and snapping shrimp, each within defined geographic radii.)

Florida Atlantic University (FAU)'s part in PALS, led by Laurent Cherubin, scrutinized subtleties in Goliath grouper communication off the South Florida coast—not far from NASA's Aquarius Reef Base, which trains astronauts sub-aqua for spaceflight—by embedding hydrophones into their habitats, using passive bioacoustic monitoring technology. That grouper are a territorial species, known to reside in and guard "limited habitat branches," as opposed to whales' or dolphins' more expansive open ocean inhabitations, make them prime candidates for surveilled study. Not technically vocalizations, a "semantic" distinction crucial for Cherubin, grouper emit low-frequency boom sounds in warning, and like other fish, they grind, stridulate, vibrate their bladders, and move their antennae in semiotic self-instrumentation. Such techniques have evolved at least thirty-three times across 34,000 species of ray-finned fishes, as opposed to a mere six times in tetrapods.[10]

To register patterns in grouper syntax under different conditions, deep-learning protocols were evolved with FAU computer scientist colleagues to "hear through" real-time variations in sound sources that included sea state, temperature, textured cross-species interaction, and sea-surface anthropophony from fishing and shipping freight.[11] One machine learning model was dubbed "Ears." Although fellow PALS scientist, Lauren Freeman of the Naval Undersea Warfare Center in Newport, described shortcomings in machine-learning applications for analyzing fish chorusing within reef environments, given that AI lacks equivalent "voice recognition" for undersea inhabitants, Cherubin's team's models proved critical in discerning what they would otherwise have had no auditory markers for. Arriving without language a priori, the model broke down inputs into features, eventually cataloguing occurrences "*in its own words* . . . in a 'machine learning space.'" Their findings, still nascent, indicate that grouper use distinct signals to identify and warn fellow fish of encroaching divers, as well as for different kinds of boats, whether cruising or fishing vessels. (Cherubin credits PALS for pushing their research into hitherto under-probed arenas and suspects that combined learnings may afford "a mine of ecological applications.")[12]

Notions of "hearing through" undersea (and sea-surface) soundscapes, now populated by industry and infrastructure space, are important when listening back to watery recordings from land, for water's high sonic metabolism platforms chatter via "orifices," both organic and synthetic, endemic and inserted. Snapping shrimps' nearly constant cavitation, where bubble collapse creates a high-intensity crackling sound to ensnare prey, produces an ambient backup track—historically treated as noise by sonar operators—in and against other distributed sound sources, often from bubble-based phenomena spread across the "fabric" mesh of H_2O itself. In sea-surface registers, individual bubbles emit milliseconds-long acoustical pulses, which oceanographer Michael Longuet-Higgins frames as "a kind of birth yell" that "choruses" in quorum oscillation.[13] An oceanic heartbeat? A glossolalic mouth?

Bubble-induced "utterance" may prove to be a useful ecological metric for assessing marine health in certain contexts, too. Linked to Lauren Freeman's research on benthic soundscapes, she, Simon Freeman, and colleagues discovered that marine macroalgae (neither plant nor animal, but protist) produce sound during photosynthesis, and that overall pitch, as a measure of algal abundance, can be an indicator of reef health.[14] Upon release into the water column, spheres of macroalgal bubbles ring, "like a bell," at the Minnaert frequency, creating a distributed sound field akin to "fizzing champagne."[15] This metabolic byproduct of photosynthesis might (I hazard) be understood as broadly phonatory—and even timescalically close in acoustic signature to those primordial, cyanobacteria-led birthscapes of photosynthesis over two billion years ago. Ones that, in deep-time "reciprocal fermentation," eventuated an atmosphere hospitable to ensuing life.[16] Such passive acoustic monitoring of macroalgal productivity may prove relevant for seaweed farming, mariculture, and carbon sequestration, and could conceivably find future application as a sensor array for PALS—moving proxies from animal realms into interstitial phyla. Could the Pacific Garbage Patch's plastic colony, of inorganic origin, be put to work in New Materialist ethos?

Such scalability in potential "deployment" among PALS's soft-tissue task forces, however, hinges upon the decryption of marine creatures' "content-rich biological signals" and the undersea spectra that inflect them, in order to become legible as "cues." Where discerned, the soniferous sociality of piscine lifeworlds starts to author informatic assemblages of extended cognition with heightened stakes, collapsing the work of *sensor* and *censor*. Dually problematic and rich in potential affordances, including as ecological assessments, the program's proposition for scientists (and technologies) to listen—first speculatively, then empirically, across zoopoetic spectrums of knowability—to how marine species sense, signal, and musick their milieus sustains an element of sonic fiction. A tinge of Arecibo. Who can tune to and transcribe these parliaments of "phonographic anticipations"?[17] Who can hear through water's many tongues, as fish listeners and *ama* divers do, and write water as water writes itself? What can bubble syntax signal of climate urgencies or mobilize as planetary imaginaries?

Seesoo, hrss, rsseeiss, ooos . . . Speech ceases.
It flows purling, widely flowing,
floating foampool, flower unfurling.[18]

NOTES

1 John Durham Peters, *The Marvelous Clouds: Towards a Philosophy of Elemental Media* (University of Chicago Press, 2016), 62.

2 Kodwo Eshun, *Adventures in Sonic Fiction: More Brilliant Than the Sun* (Quartet Books, 1998), 00[-001].

3 J.-P. Caron and Patricia Reed, "Listening to Unencoded Worlds," in *Sound – Space – Sense*, ed. Detlef Diedrichsen et al. (Spector Books, 2022), 25.

4 Emma McCormick Goodhart, "Underwater (Un)Sound," *e-flux Architecture* (August 2020), https://www.e-flux.com/architecture/oceans/341778/underwater-un-sound/.

5 Lendl Barcelos, "The Nuclear Sonic: Listening to Millennial Matter," in *Aesthetics After Finitude*, ed. Amy Ireland et al. (re.press, 2016), 71–88.

6 "Special Notice (SN) DARPA-SN-18-29: Persistent Aquatic Living Sensors (PALS) Proposers Day," accessed December 27, 2024, https://imlive.s3.amazonaws.com/Federal Government/ID376656389797512793551977352629105669294/DARPA-SN-18-29_FINAL.pdf; https://www.darpa.mil/news/2019/detect-undersea-activity.

7 My conversations with DARPA PALS-funded scientists Laurent Cherubin, Lauren Freeman, and Alison Laferriere form the basis, in large part, of my understanding of the program.

8 and 9 Lauren Freeman, personal interview, December 27, 2024.

10 Rachel Teng Ruiqi, "The Ocean Is a Cacophony of Fish Talk, Study Shows. We Just Can't Hear It," Mongabay, March 30, 2022, https://news.mongabay.com/2022/03/the-ocean-is-a-cacophony-of-fish-talk-study-shows-we-just-cant-hear-it/.

11 I develop notions of "hearing through" matter in my chapter, "At the Edge of the Audible: Auscultating Non-Auditory Geographies," in *Articulating Media: Genealogy, Interface, Situation*, ed. James Gabrillo and Nathaniel Zetter (Open Humanities Press, 2023).

12 Laurent Cherubin, personal interview, January 4, 2025.

13 M. S. Longuet-Higgins, "Bubble Noise Mechanisms: A Review," in *Natural Physical Sources of Underwater Sound*, ed. B. R. Kerman (Kluwer Academic Publishers, 1993).

14 Simon E. Freeman et al., "Photosynthesis by Marine Algae Produces Sound, Contributing to the Daytime Soundscape on Coral Reefs," *PLoS ONE* 13, no. 10 (2018): e0201766.

15 Sarah Keartes, "Photosynthesis Makes a Sound," *Hakai Magazine*, November 29, 2018, https://hakaimagazine.com/news/photosynthesis-makes-a-sound/.

16 Emanuele Coccia's remarks in his reading "Philosophy of the Home," Swiss Institute, May 12, 2024.

17 Fred Moten, *In the Break: The Aesthetics of the Black Radical Tradition* (University of Minnesota Press, 2003), 11.

18 James Joyce, *Ulysses* (Vintage International, 1990), 49.

Sonic Investigations

Valentin Bansac, Ludwig Berger, Mike Fritsch,
Alice Loumeau & Peter Szendy

[December 23, 2024, 9:54 AM]

Dear Ludwig,

... I have heard lots of things about your recordings for the Luxembourg Pavilion at the Venice Biennale. I have also read the field notes Alice made during your trip together through various sites. I am eager to know more about them. I have so many questions ...

Let's start, maybe, with this one: What kind of equipment did you carry with you? I remember that you talked about the various microphones you used as "instruments in an orchestra": Could you describe them and say more about this orchestral dimension?

I would like to meet them one by one and be able to think about them as musicians.

Warmly,
Peter

[December 28, 2024, 12:07 PM]

Dear Peter,

. . . Yes, I like to think of my microphones as musical instruments that are "played" by the beings, elements, and objects in an environment. A passing car, for example, will "play" each microphone differently, with its sound entangled in each microphone's unique characteristics. Just as traditional instruments have unique frequency ranges, timbres, characters, and directionalities, so too do these microphones. Together, they form a kind of "microphone orchestra," with different sections contributing their distinct voices to the overall composition.

This orchestra includes four microphones for vibrations (structure-borne sounds), ten microphones for airborne sound, two hydrophones (for waterborne sounds), and three sensors for electromagnetic waves. Let me introduce them to you, section by section.

Vibrational Section
This section focuses on the tactile world of sound, capturing vibrations that travel through solid objects. It brings weight and depth to the ensemble. These microphones are "played" by the materials themselves, uncovering the hidden resonances of structures, surfaces, and even the vibrational communication of animals (biotremology).

Geophone (LOM Geofón): Specializes in deep bass frequencies, delivering a full, powerful sound while muffling the higher frequencies. It can be "played" by vibrations in the ground or through attachment to structures like metal bridges. Originally designed for World War I mine warfare, I now use it to explore the resonances of large objects in the environment.

Laser Doppler Vibrometer (Polytec VibroGo): Uses a laser beam to detect vibrations in reflective surfaces, allowing fragile objects like blades of grass to "play" it. Its extreme sensitivity uncovers even the tiniest vibrations. Originally developed as a Soviet spy tool, I mostly use it to eavesdrop on insect communication through plants.

Contact mic 1 (AKG C411): This mic has a warm, rounded sound and focuses on low and mid frequencies. It was designed for string instruments, giving it a musical quality I enjoy, especially when attached to machines or resonant surfaces.

Contact mic 2 (Schertler DYN UNI P48): Similar to the AKG, but "cleaner" and more detailed. It reveals finer textures and details but sounds sometimes a bit thinner than the other contact mic.

Airborne Section

This section is "played" by sounds traveling through the air, from winds and birds to the deep hum of distant traffic.

IRT Cross (4 × Neumann 140): Four microphones arranged in a square, "played" equally by sounds from all directions. It creates a balanced and realistic representation of the environment, anchoring all other microphone signals in a coherent sound image.

AB Omnidirectional Pair (2 × Nevaton MC 590): Placed directly on the ground to pick up deeper sounds and add an earthy texture. These are sometimes "played" by critters moving across the surface.

Flexible Omnidirectional Pair (2 × LOM Uši Pro): Lightweight and versatile, I often place these in small holes or crevices to record hidden sound worlds and resonances. Adds a very close, detailed perspective to the ensemble.

Parabolic (Telinga Modular): Highly directional, focusing on mid and high frequencies while lacking deeper frequencies. Ideal to be played by faint or distant sounds like birds or power lines.

Hydrophone Section

"Played" through water, this section reveals rich underwater soundscapes such as subtle water movements, water insects, or photosynthesizing underwater plants.

Hydrophone Pair (2 × ASF1 MKII): These hydrophones are very sensitive, translating aquatic vibrations into clear, nuanced sound. Unlike clichéd muffled underwater recordings, they also capture beautifully rich high frequencies.

Electromagnetic Section
This section is "played" by the invisible electromagnetic fields generated by infrastructure, such as electrical grids, communication towers, and electronic devices, as well as by natural electromagnetic phenomena.

Electromagnetic Sensor Pair (2 × LOM Elektrouši): These sensors have a short range, but a nice stereo field. They work best when used very close to the objects, making them ideal to be played by small machines.

Magnetic Antenna (LOM Priezor): Less focused but with a broader range, this antenna is played by the larger electromagnetic fields of a space, revealing the ambient electrical environment.

In most cases, I record the same environment simultaneously with many of these microphones, each capturing a different facet of the space. Later, I mix the recordings—much like a conductor shaping an orchestra, to create a balanced sonic image—emphasize specific details, and offer a multidimensional experience of the environment.

I hope this gives you a sense of the orchestral dimension I think about when using my microphones in the field. . . .

Warmly,
Ludwig

[January 2, 2025, 6:42 PM]

Thank you so much, dear Ludwig, for this wonderful introduction to your "orchestra." I couldn't help thinking that what you are describing is a twenty-first-century equivalent of an *Orchestration Treatise* like Berlioz's, with sections divided not into strings or brass but into vibrational types. Fascinating.

Since you extended the orchestral metaphor (if it is simply a metaphor) to include yourself as a conductor, I would like to ask you: How did you plan and then conduct the performance of the field recordings in the various sites that you visited with Alice, Mike, and Valentin? Were there specific challenges or, to stay with our orchestral analogy, were there especially difficult passages that you had to rehearse repeatedly?

[January 10, 2025, 12:59 PM]

Dear Peter,

Thank you for your observation and for drawing the connection to Berlioz's *Orchestration Treatise*. I read a bit of it after your comment, and I agree—it's a fascinating parallel!

My approach to field recording is usually spontaneous and small-scale. I spend long periods in one place exploring different spatial and temporal perspectives. For me, field recording is a slow dialogue: the place offers its voices, I respond by adjusting my microphones, and the site answers with new sounds. This process can feel endless.

Working on this project with Alice, Mike, and Valentin was a completely new experience in terms of scale and space. We explored around ten main locations spread across a vast, interconnected landscape. This turned the place we were recording into the entire territory, which of course made the logistics much more complicated. We revisited locations at different times to find the moments when the place revealed both its variety as well as its most characteristic sounds—early mornings at lakes and forests (for the birds), evenings in meadows (for the insects), and late nights for data centers (for the 24/7 hum). Using our large ensemble of microphones added to the complexity. Setting up took time, and sound is always fleeting—like a murmuration of starlings that vanished before we could finish setting up. To capture what we couldn't record immediately, we left weatherproof wildlife recorders in some locations for up to several months.

Some places offered a richer palette of sounds than others. At the lake with floating solar panels, for example, there was an abundance of textures: floating plastic, underwater photosynthesis, humming machines, electromagnetic activity, distant industrial and train sounds, birds on the lake, and wind in the reeds. By contrast, a power plant with the loud constant noise from pump generators was much more challenging. I had to focus on the details—how the vibrations from the noise resonated through materials like metal tubes, doors, and rails. I am always more interested in listening *through* rather than just listening *to*—like sensing car vibrations through the metal of a lake dam bridge, rather than the cars themselves; like experiencing a meadow from the perspective of a grasshopper.

In the end, the process comes down to three key decisions: when, where, and how to record exactly. Combined, these choices open up endless possibilities, and so perhaps the biggest challenge for me is always to decide when to stop recording and move on to the next site.

Best,
Ludwig

[January 24, 2025, 4:45 PM]

Dear Ludwig, Peter,

We're jumping in after joyfully reading your rich conversation about field recording instruments and protocols.

Ludwig, we became acquainted with your recording process on-site, as we hiked and investigated the many locations together in Luxembourg, but we are less familiar with the process of composition. Could you describe this specific moment of your work, post site investigation, in the studio? How do you compose the recordings (the many hours of recordings) into a narrative? How much does your embodied experience of field recording inform the composition? Since we thought of a storyline together in Luxembourg, we were wondering how much freedom you take, in general, in creating, layering, and assembling a final sound piece from its point of departure.

Speak very soon,
Alice, Mike, and Valentin

[February 9, 2025, 11:23 PM]

Dear all,

Thank you for your further questions. After our recordings in Luxembourg, I began by distributing the recordings according to the sequence we had outlined during our trip. In my notes, I wrote:

Morning lake: birds and cars
Photovoltaic lake: photosynthesis, floating plastic, electromagnetics
Dam outside: wall acoustics, cars
Dam inside: metal resonances
Switchgear: electricity
Wind turbine: chord, open landscape
Satellite park: noise swells, birds (+ starlings) and insects, vibroscape
Meadow: afternoon and night
Data centers: hums and night insects
Highway (close-up)
Forest: highway, transition to day

From this overall structure, I worked in stages, moving from a broad layout to finer details. First, I arranged the central recordings of each location into a rough sequence, covering the full thirty-minute duration. Then, I gradually added more layers—similar to orchestration—building up density and connections between sounds. Here you can find a screenshot of one of my projects, where up to ten recordings play in parallel.

I process the recordings in two main ways: through filtering and speed adjustments. Filtering allows me to isolate specific elements or tonalities or to clarify voices within noisier recordings, while speed adjustments reveal tonal or rhythmic structures that might otherwise be imperceptible. I take certain liberties in shaping the piece musically but always with the aim of preserving the presence of the place itself. For me, the recordings are not just raw material to be manipulated freely, each sound should say something specific about the location or its context. This also guides my overall selection: I primarily layer only sounds recorded on the same site, preserving their relationships and coexistence. Only rarely do I incorporate sounds from other moments to support the piece's overall form and narrative.

But one of the main challenges in field recording is that a recording rarely captures how a place actually felt. Perception in the field is multisensory, and the act of listening is entangled with movement, spatial awareness, smells, the cultural and historical context, and so on. In the composition, I try to reconstruct and translate these experiences, which leads to a process of place-remaking. This also involves emphasizing what makes each location sonically distinct—sometimes by bringing certain sounds or certain aspects of sounds into the foreground.

A key aspect of this piece was highlighting the connections between anthropogenic sounds (human-made, directly or indirectly) and biophonic sounds (produced by animals and plants). For example, electromagnetic recordings and insect sounds were strikingly similar, sometimes indistinguishable. These connections became even more apparent when adjusting playback speed—certain insect calls or electromagnetic vibrations only revealed their structure when slowed down.

This approach also reflects how different species perceive time. A bird, for instance, hears its own song in a completely different temporal framework than we do. So, what is the true speed of a bird's song?

Sometimes, I layer different speeds of the same sound, allowing it to be heard from multiple acoustic perspectives at once. This multiperspectival approach is central to all stages of my soundscape composition—not just in how I record (using various microphones) but also in how I compose. I do tell a story and guide the ear, highlighting different aspects, but I like to keep the soundscape open, so the listener can move through it freely and shift their focus.

Best,
Ludwig

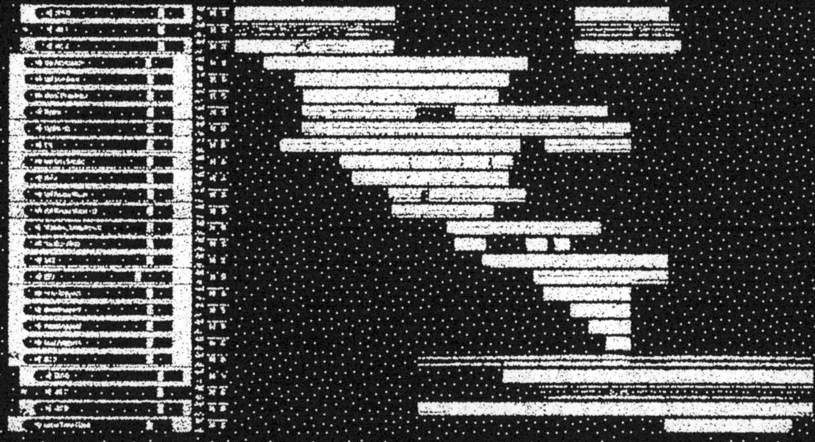

Postproduction process, Ludwig Berger

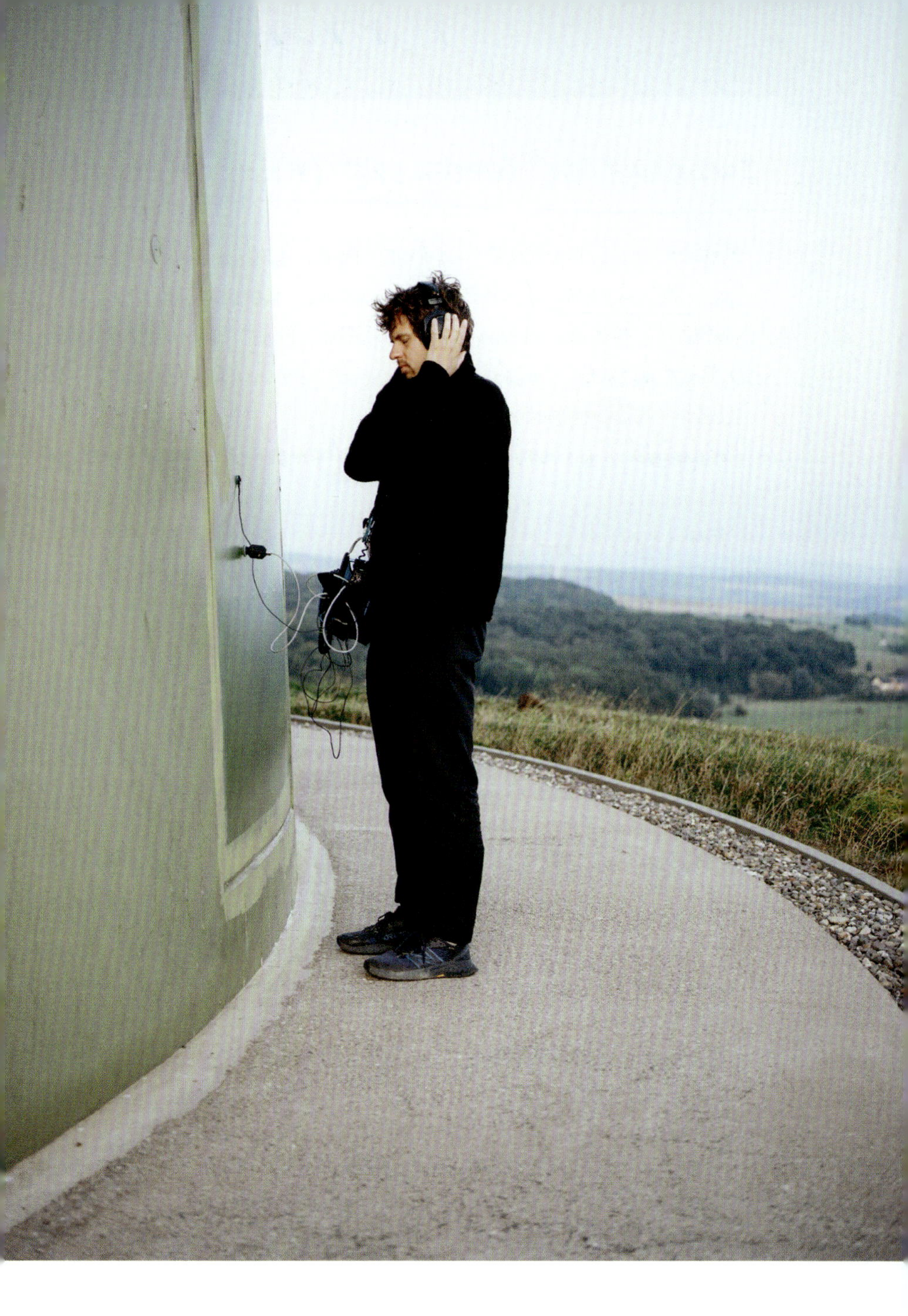

SATURDAY 21 SEPTEMBRE (FIRST DAY OF THE FA

= EARLY MORNING SPOT FOR BIRD HEARING IN REMICHE (THE NATURAL RESERVE)

- SPOT: ON A SMALL WOODEN PLATFORM ON THE LAK ON THE OTHER SIDE OF THE WOODEN HUT FROM LAST TIME (TUESDAY)
- AROUND 6:15 TO 7:20 (END OF BIRD ACTION)
- EQUIP.

* A BIRD PHOTOGRA WAS ALSO AT THE SP (VERY SERIOUS LOOKI

→ ON THE WOODEN BALUSTRADE

- WEATHER: MORNING CHILL + SUN COMING OUT, BEAUTIFUL MORNING LIGHT, REFLECTION ON THE WATER
- WORDS. SOUNDS: CHORUS / INTENSITY / DIMMED / VOICE
  GENARAL: CRAWLING / CALM / FOGGY / CHOREOGRA

= STOP 2 - IN NIEDERANVEN (NATUUR RESERVE) TO LISTEN TO THE INSECTS AGAIN AT THE SAME S THAN WEDNESDAY IN DAY LIGHT
11:00 AM
- EQUIP

X

CRICKETS / INSECTS

GEO PHONE

ATMOS

EATHER - , SUNNY, BRIGHT, WARM
SOUNDS - VERY QUIET, SOME BIRDS, SOME CRIQUETS, AIRPLANES IN THE BACK + ROADS

WORDS - SOUND = MUFFLED / ECHO / REPETITIVE
GENERAL = HEAT / SUN LIGHT / HOT

SPOT 3 - ESCH-SUR-SÛRE DAM, ON TOP OF THE DAM ROAD -

MICS

SPOT -

EQUIP

VIBRATION CARS

GEOPHONE

CONTACT MIC

+

OVER BOARD THE DAM WALL

- WEATHER = SUNNY, CONTRASTY, BLUE SKY, LIGHT BREEZE
- SOUNDS = SWOOSHING CARS, TOURIST, FEW BIRDS
- WORDS - SOUND = SUSTAINED / SWOOSH / LOUD / FULL
GENERAL = GREEN / IN-BETWEEN / LIMINAL / CAGE

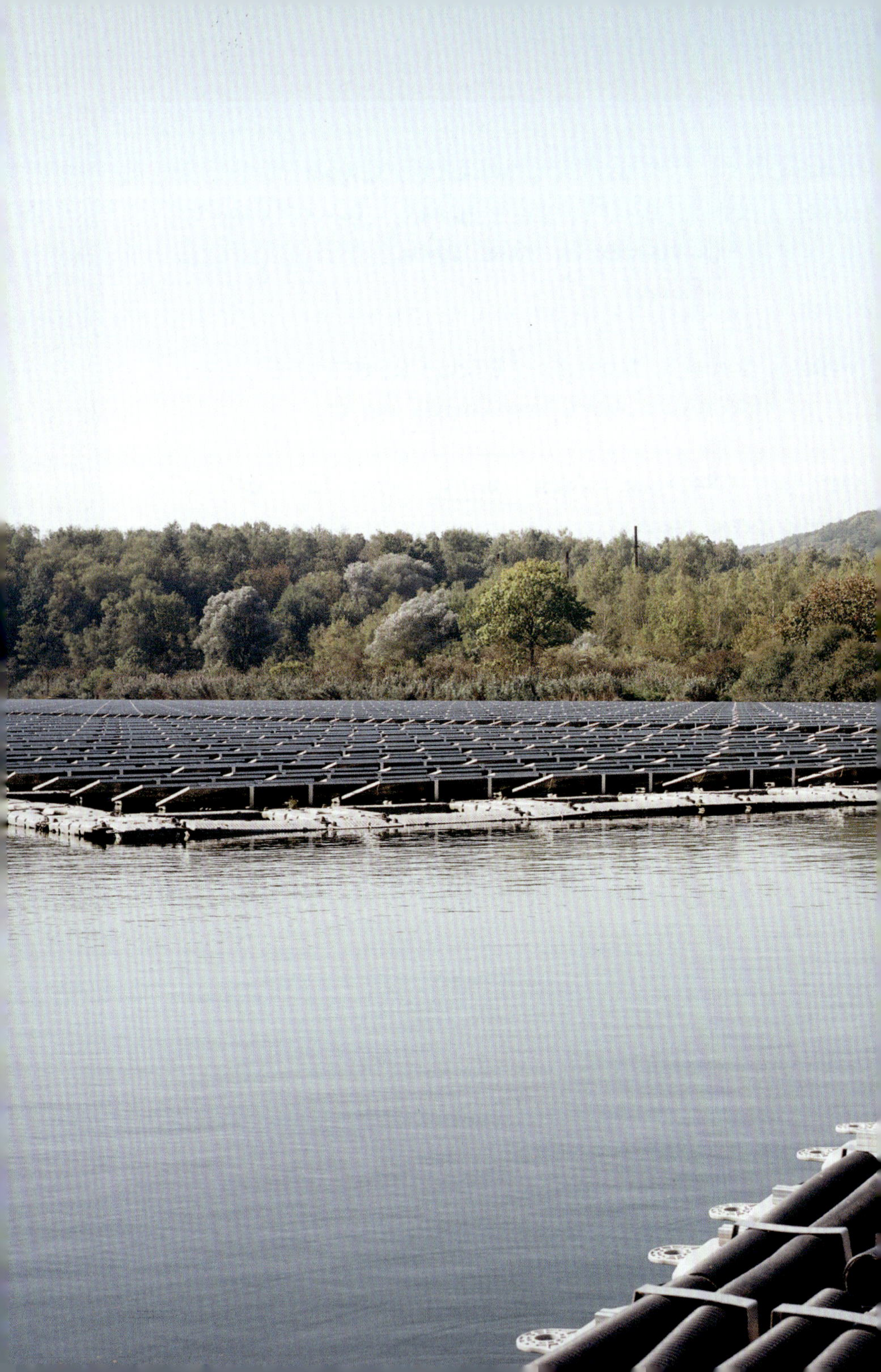

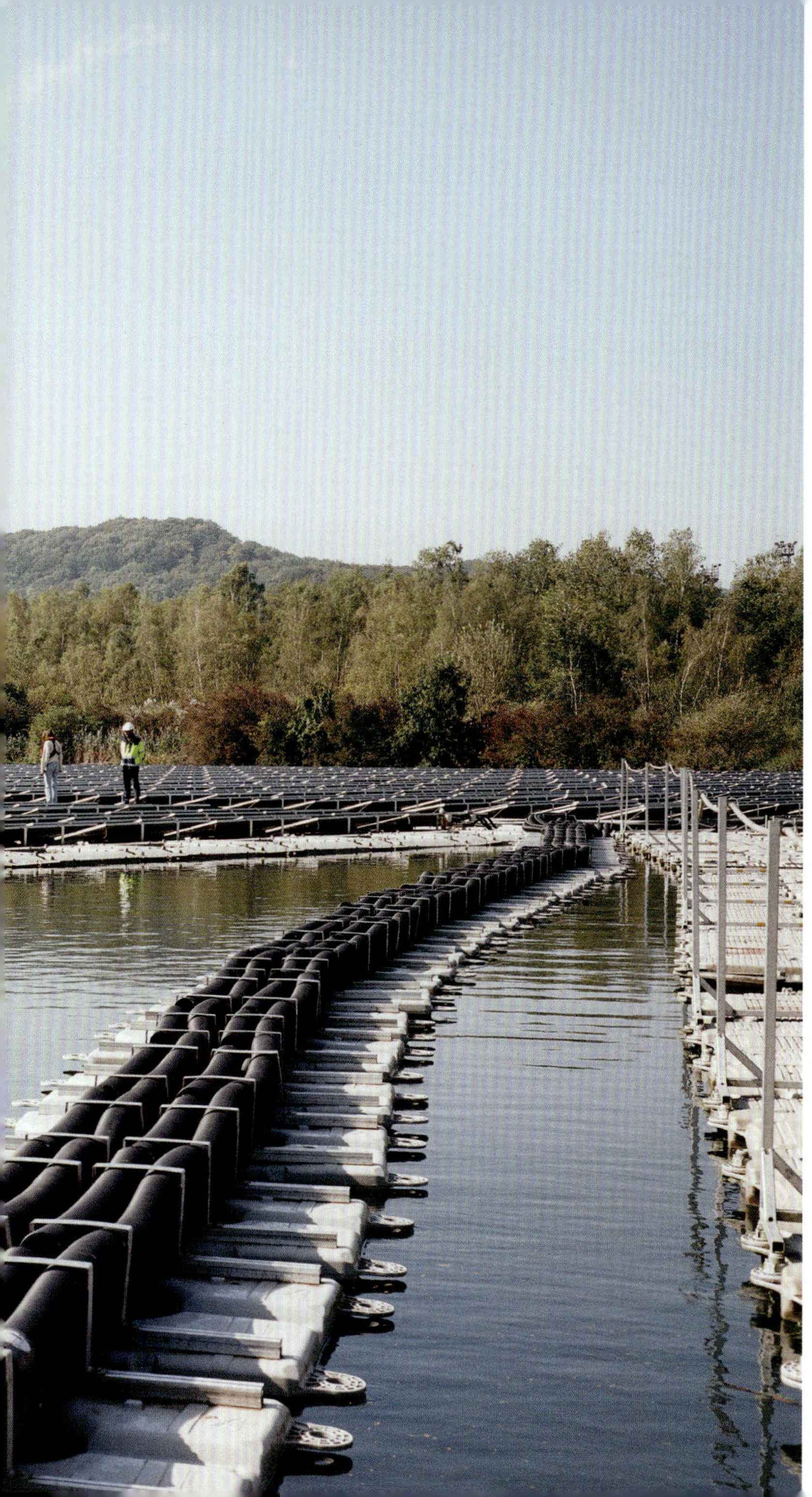

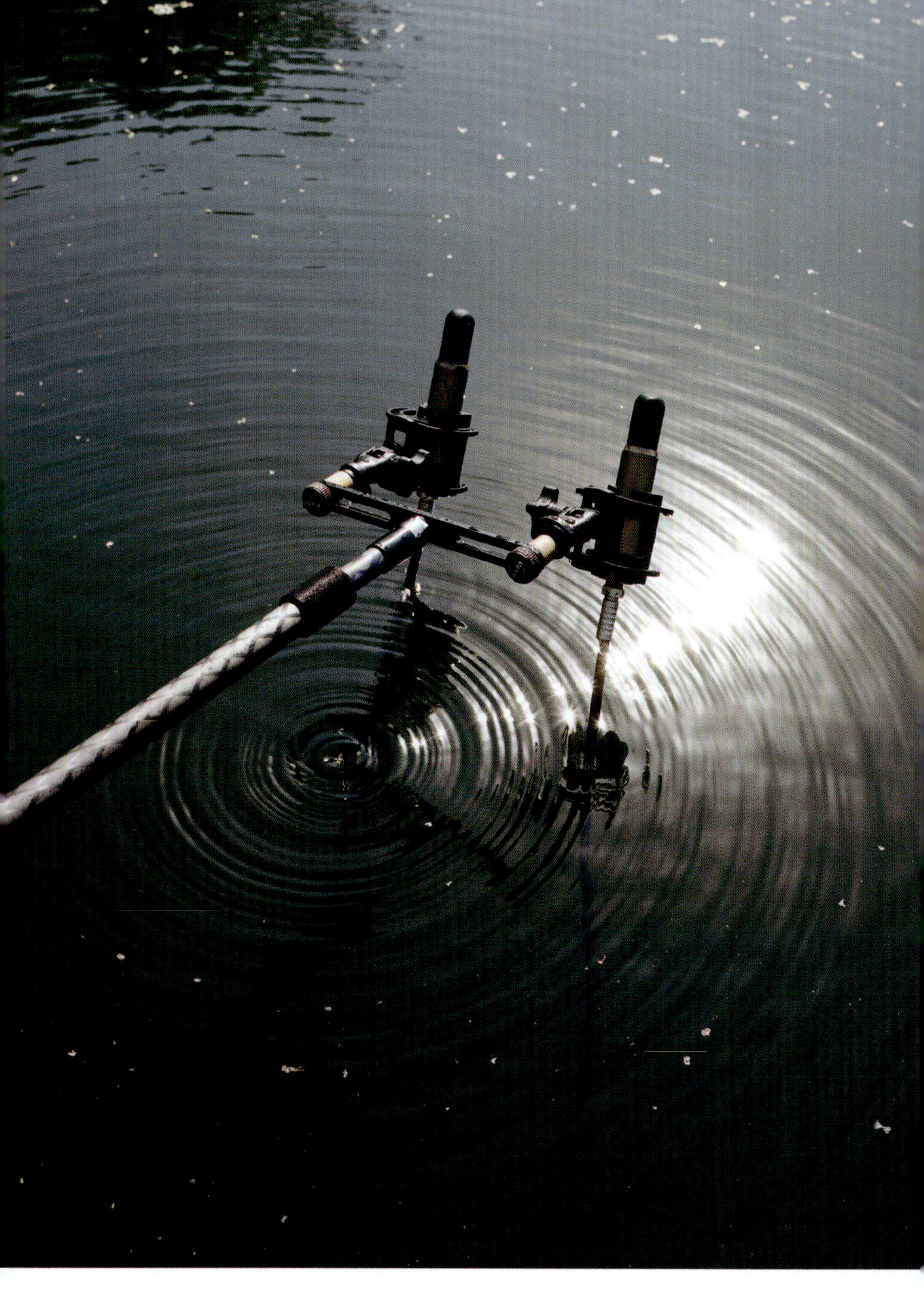

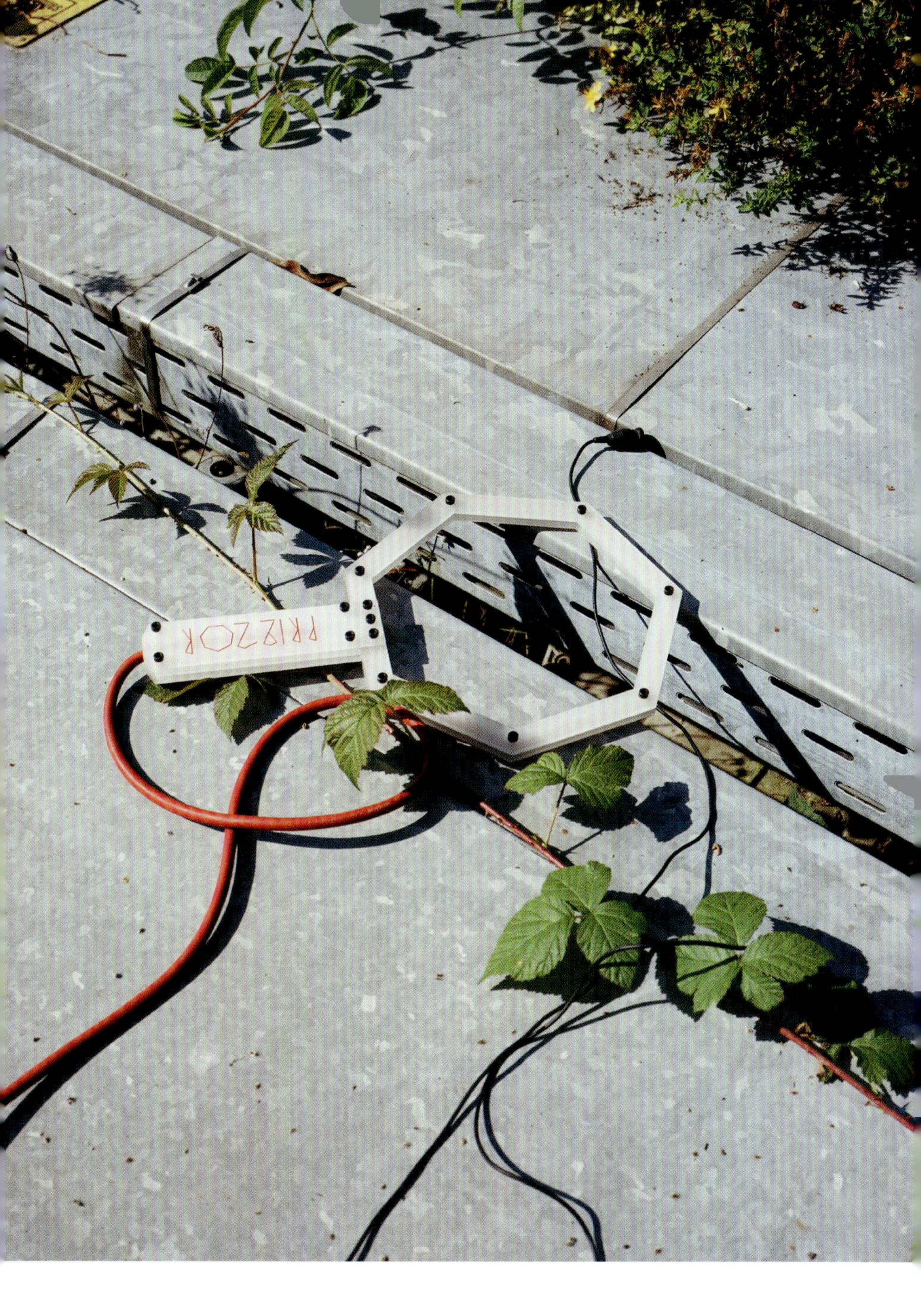

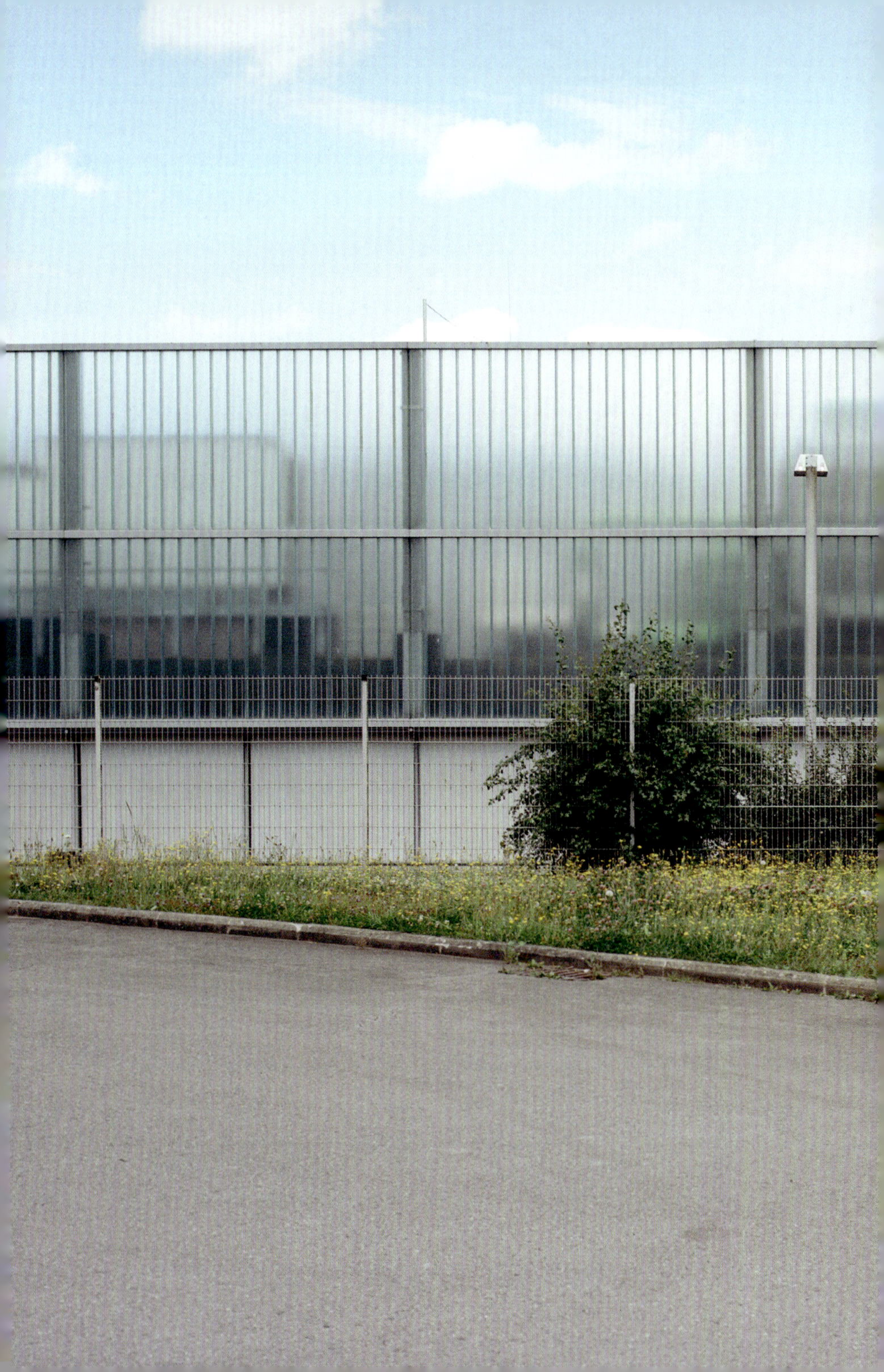

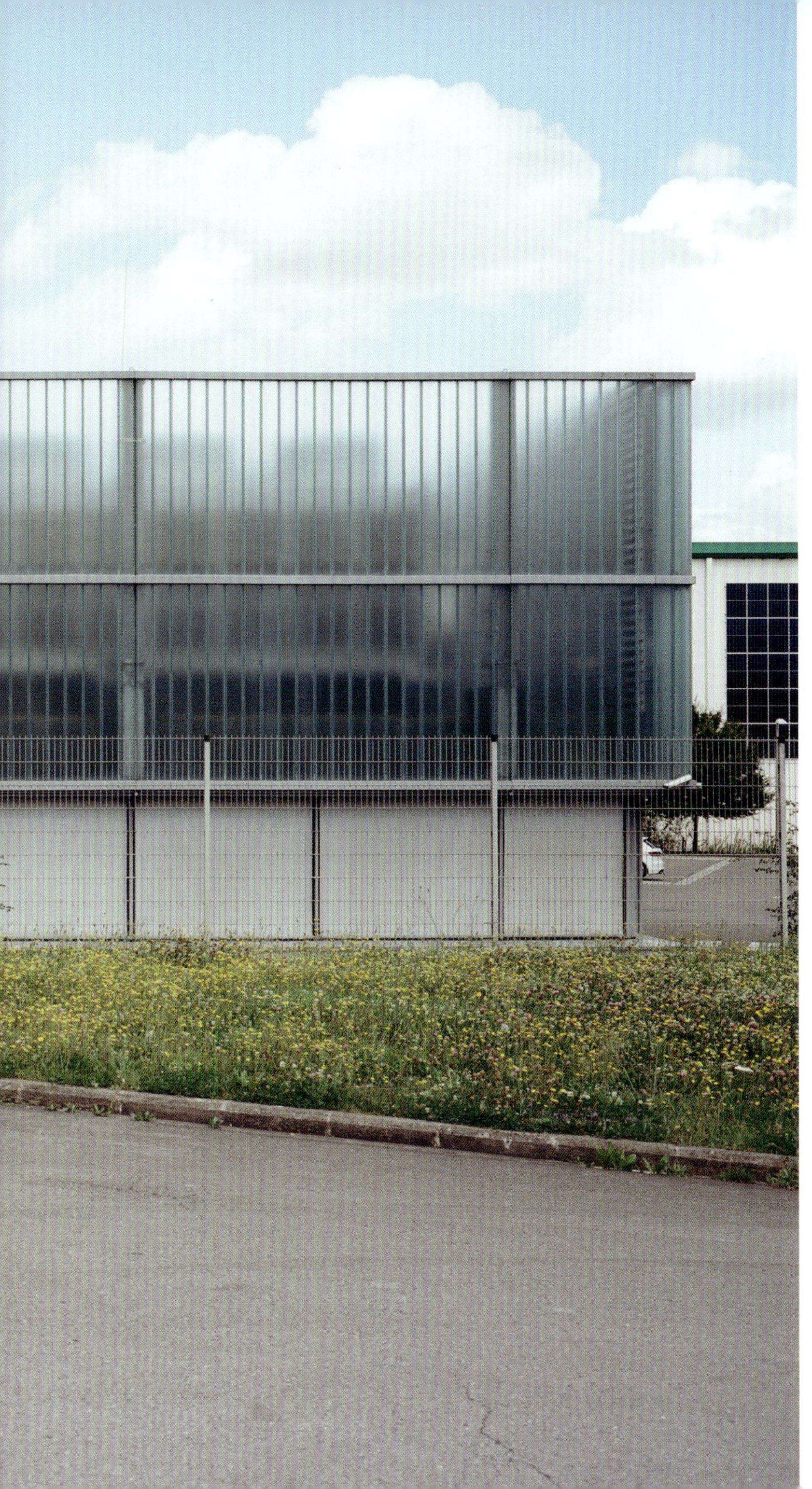

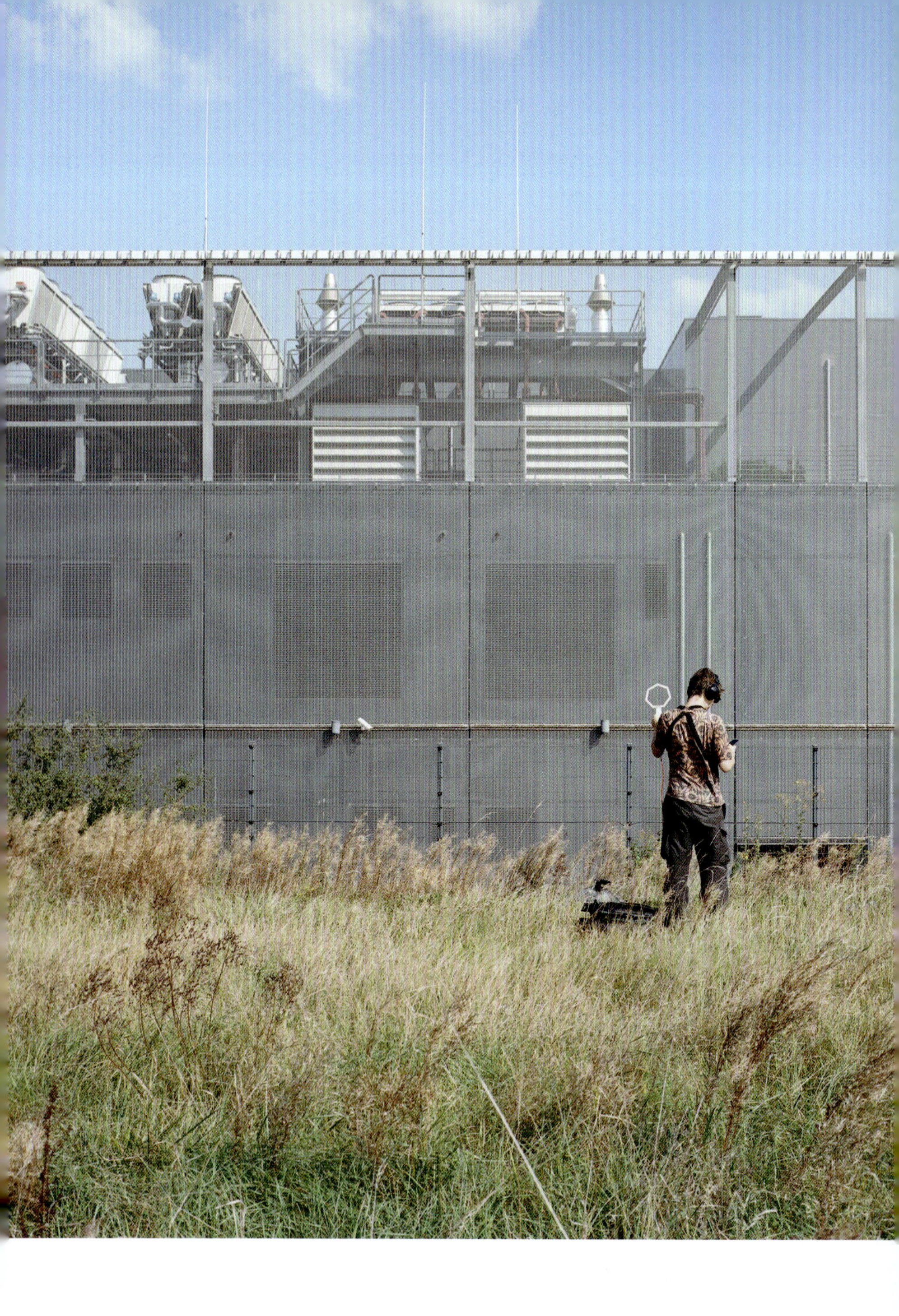

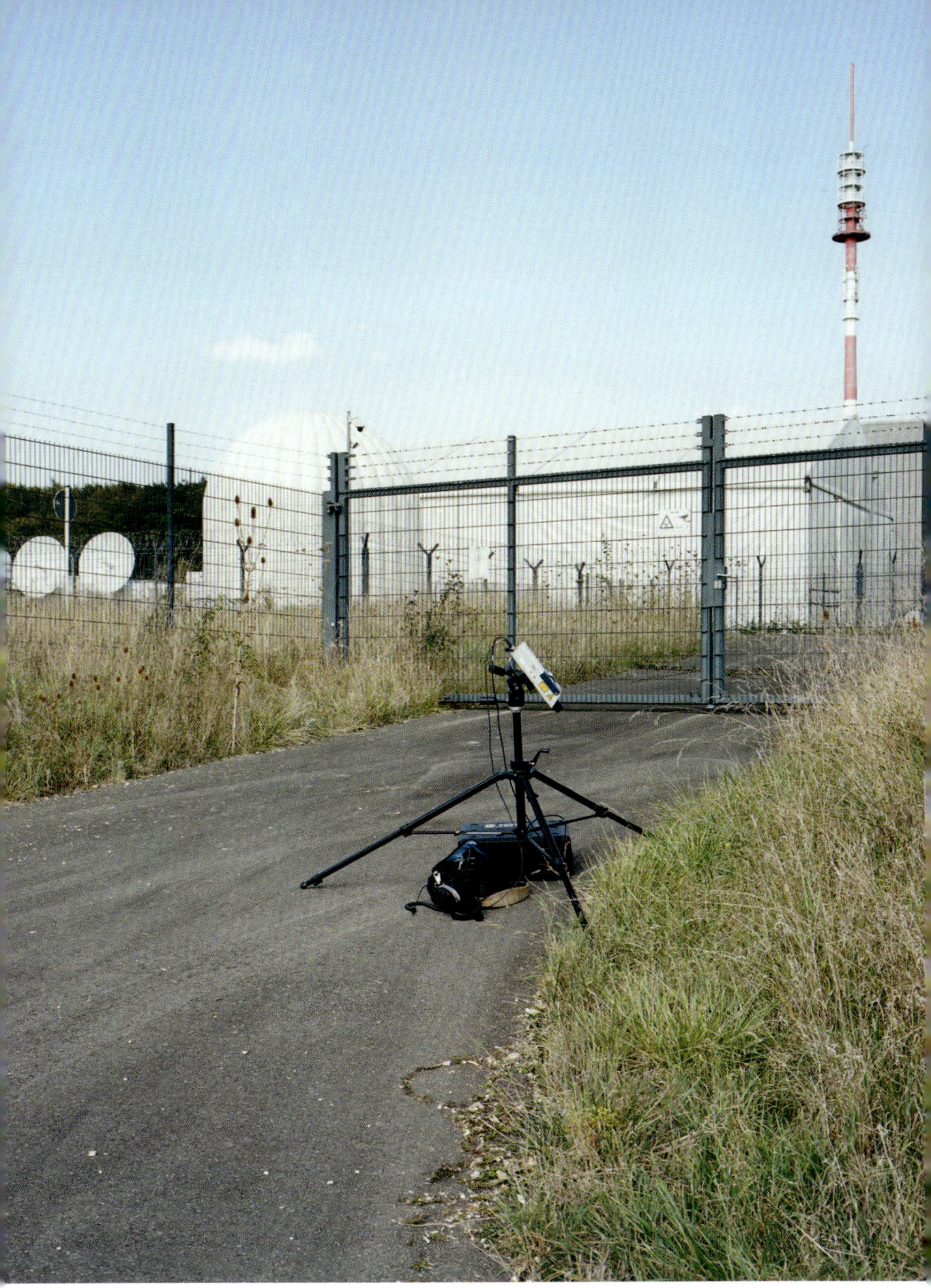

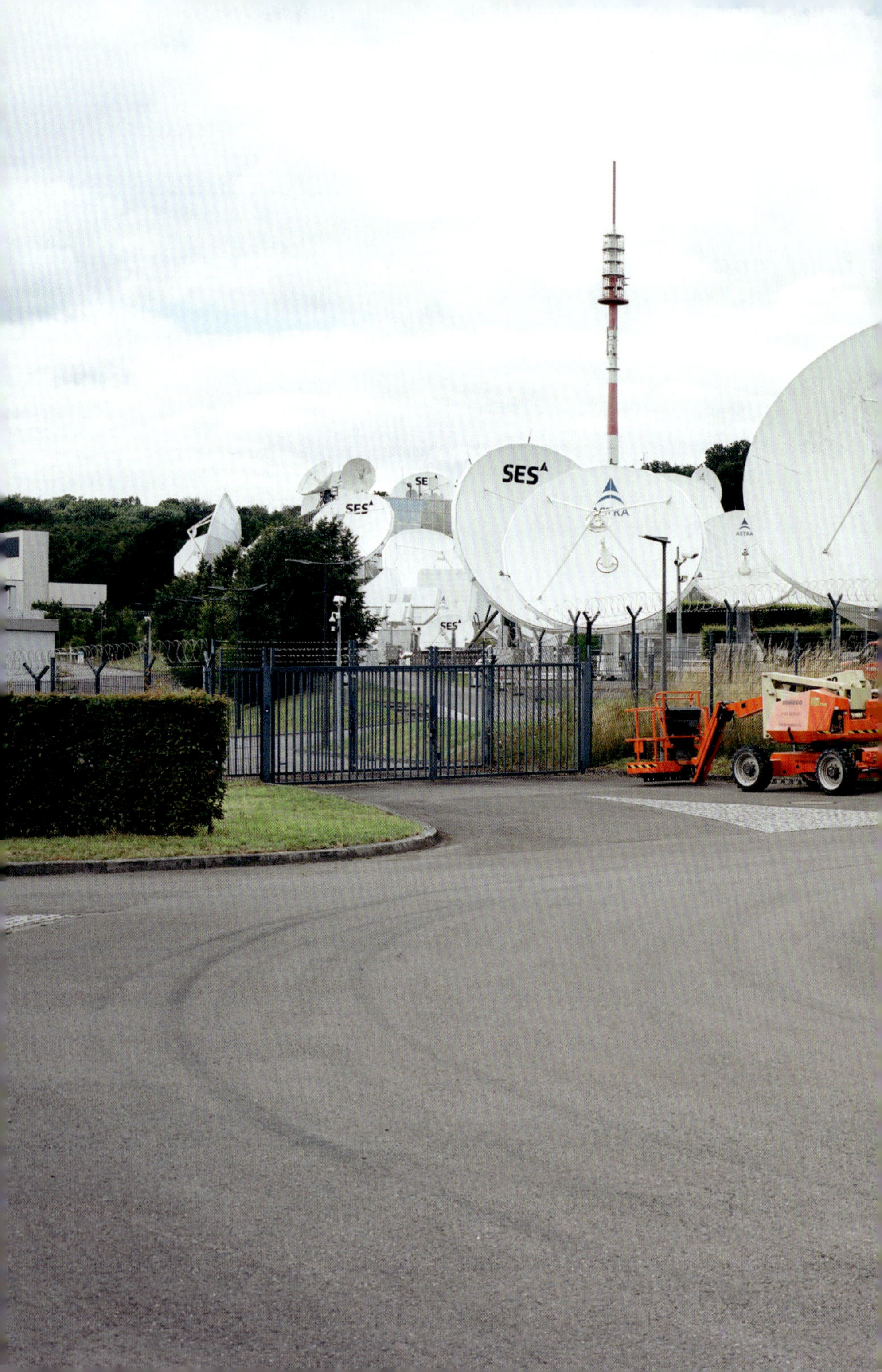
SES
SES
ASTRA
ASTRA
SES

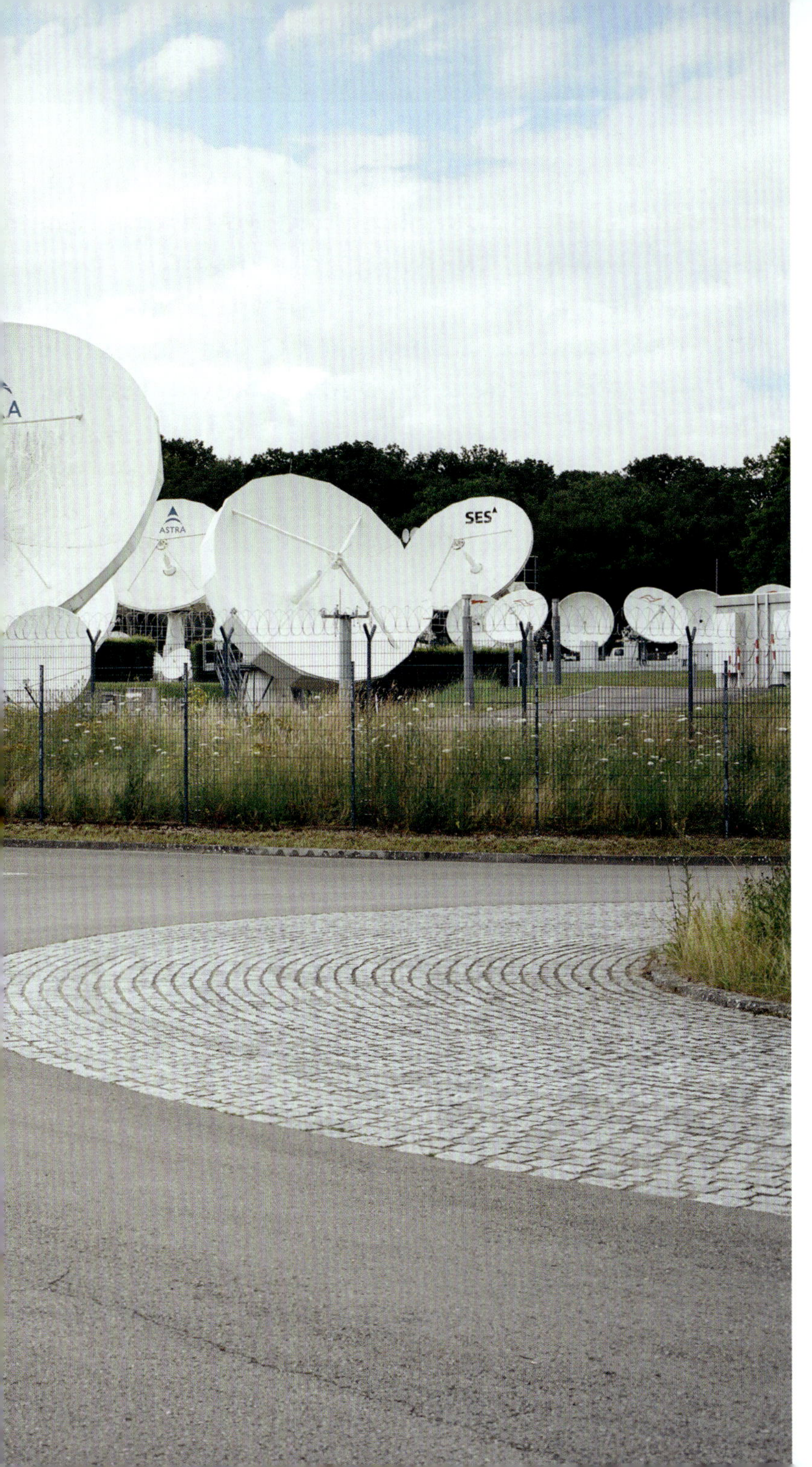
ASTRA
SES

HIGH CORN FIELD, TALLER THAN US, ALIGNED IN PERFECT LINES. THEY ECHO THE PLACEMENT OF T[illegible] PARABOLS IN FRONT. THE FRICTION BETWE[illegible] THE LEAVES MAKES A SORT OF ECHO ALL AROUN[illegible] ME. I AM SITTING ALONE WITH THE MICS DOWN ON THE FIELD FLOOR. IT FEELS LIKE GHOSTS ALL AROUND. SOFT TOUCHING – THE SUN IS SHINING THROUGH THE STEMS BUT QUICKLY COVERED BY THICK CLOUDS. END OF CORN MEDITATIONS.

EQUIP –

BOTH ON THE FLOOR

INSIDE THE FIELD, LOWER THAN CORN STEMS

WORDS = SOUND = GHOSTS / HANDS / LEAVES / WAVES.
GENERAL – PLACEMENT / PLANT – PEOPLE / FALLIN[illegible]
CORNY.

= DRIVE TO <u>RASCHPËTZER</u>, FOREST.

WATER RETENTION STRATEGY / FOREST REGENERATION PROJECT, PONDS, MOSSY FLOOR.

EQUIP =

WORDS = SOUNDS = BUBBLY / SPACIOUS / DEATH / SQUISHY
GENERAL = MOSSY / MICROS[illegible]
SOFT NESS / PILLOWS

DRIVE TO PARKPLATZ. A BRIDGE / PLATFORM WHERE TUNNEL FROM HIGHWAY DIVES INTO THE GROUND (A7). FENCED ACCESS – NO RECORDINGS...

DRIVE TO GRUNEWALD. WHERE WE PLACED THE SONG METER OVER THE SUMMER. IN THE SAME FOREST AREA. ATMOS RECORDING.

EQUIP =

BOTH SMALL MICS (AERIAL)

ON LOGS

MEDITATION SEQUENCE, WE ARE ALL SITTING ON A LOG IN AN ARRAY.

WORDS = SOUNDS: DRONE / BASS / CONTINUITY / QUIET.
GENERAL: CATHEDRAL / ENERGY / FLOW / PEACEFUL.

- ON THE WAY BACK TO THE CAR. STOP ALONG THE ROAD BETWEEN THE FOREST AND TRAM LUX DEPOT. THIS IN-BETWEEN SPACE IS AN ECOTONE!
SOUNDS = TRAM*, ROAD, CHATTERS, CITY DRONE, PLANES, INSECTS, WIND IN BRANCHES. * METAL RAILINGS, BIKES...
BIRDS (⊖)

EQUIP =

TOWARD THE FOREST

WORDS = SOUNDS = RATTLES / URBAN /

GENERAL = ECOTONE /

MOBILITY /

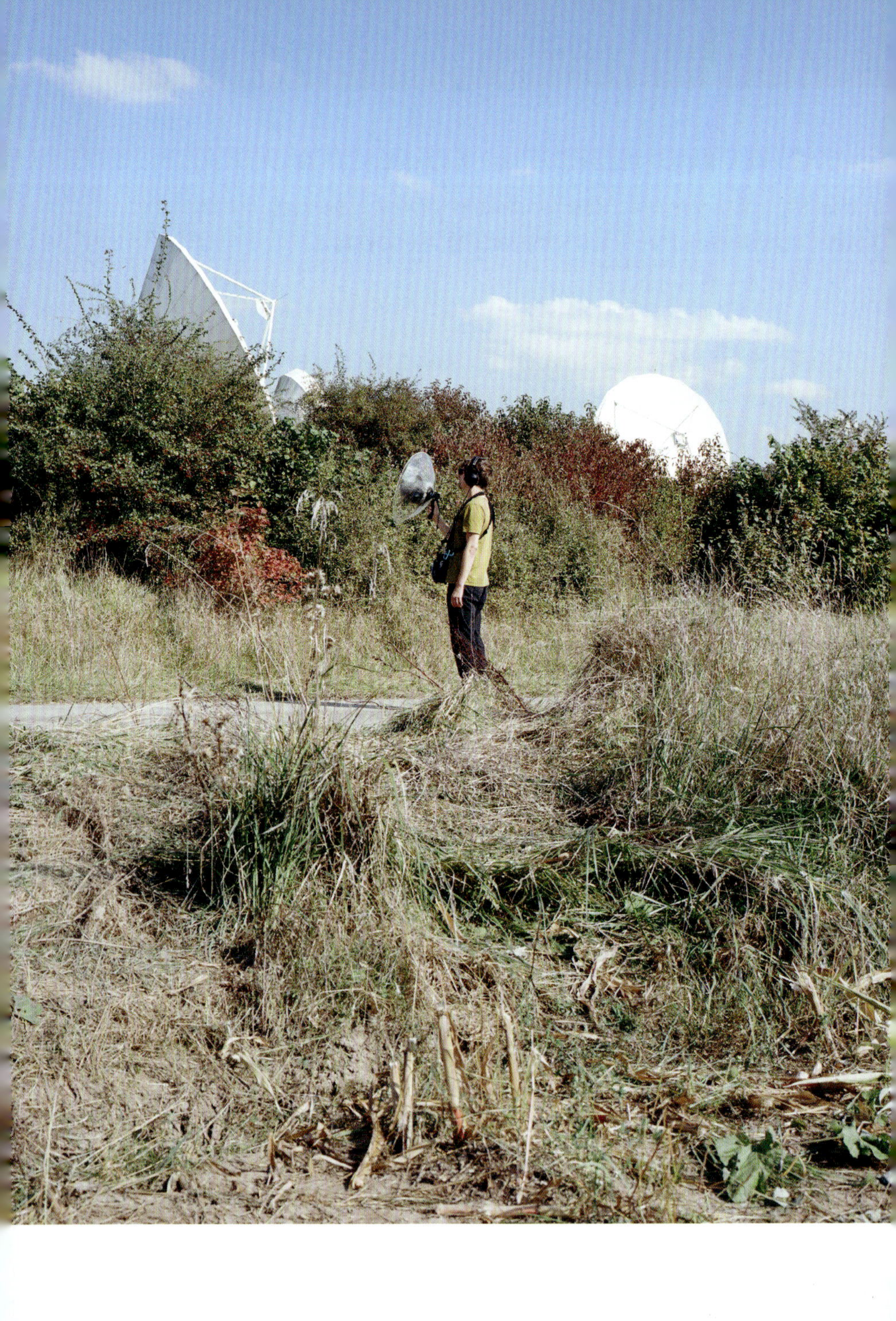

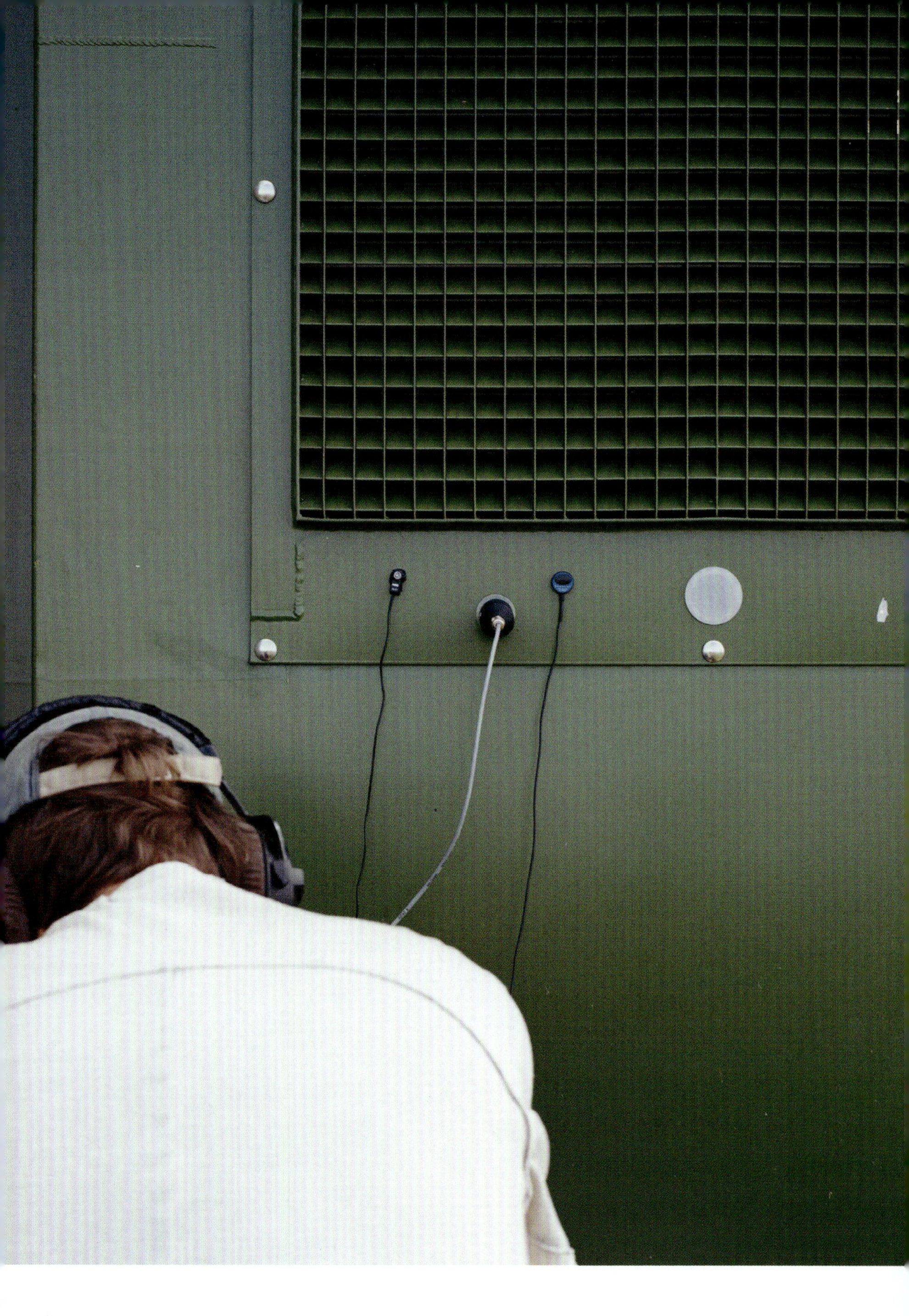

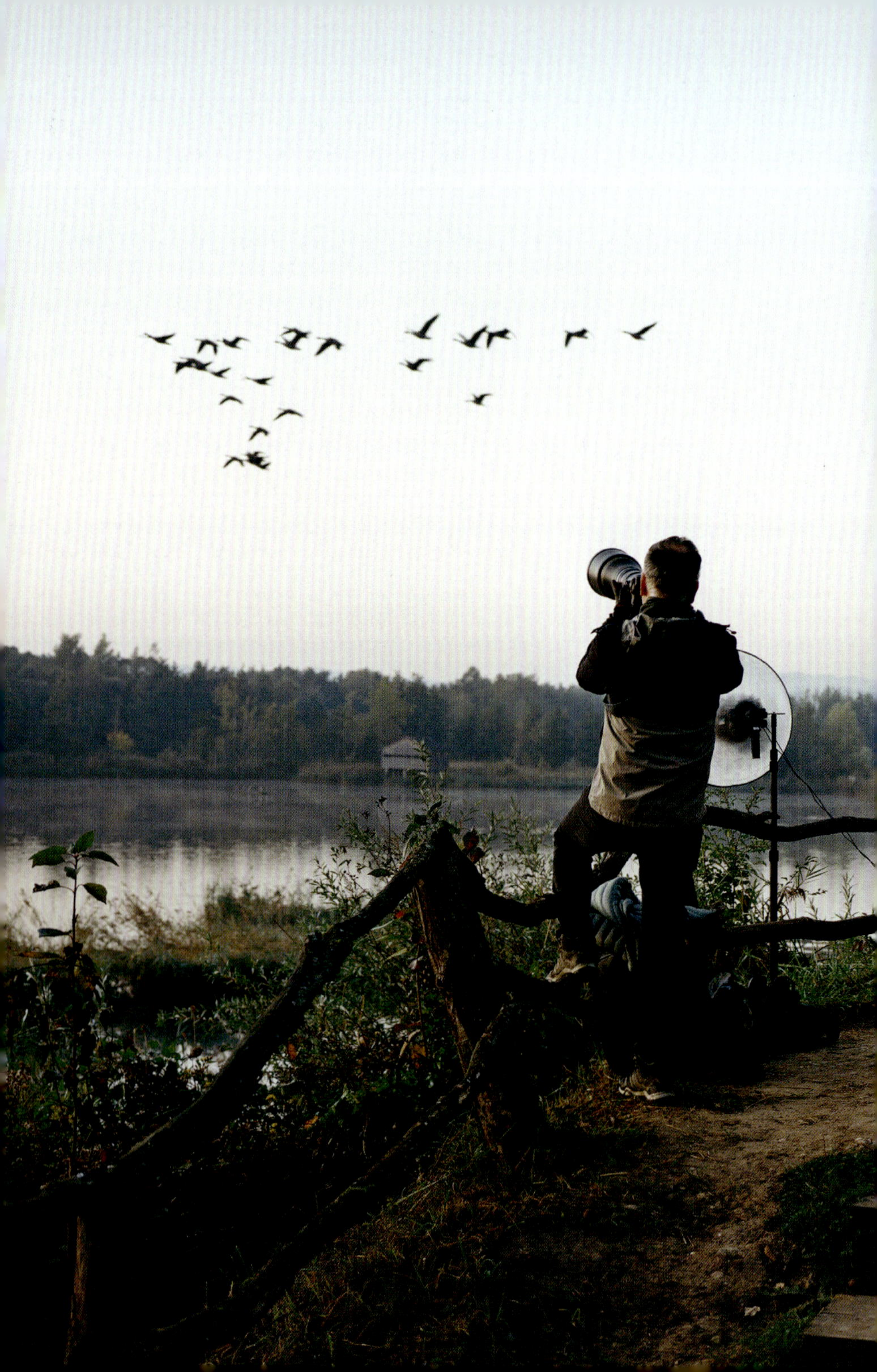

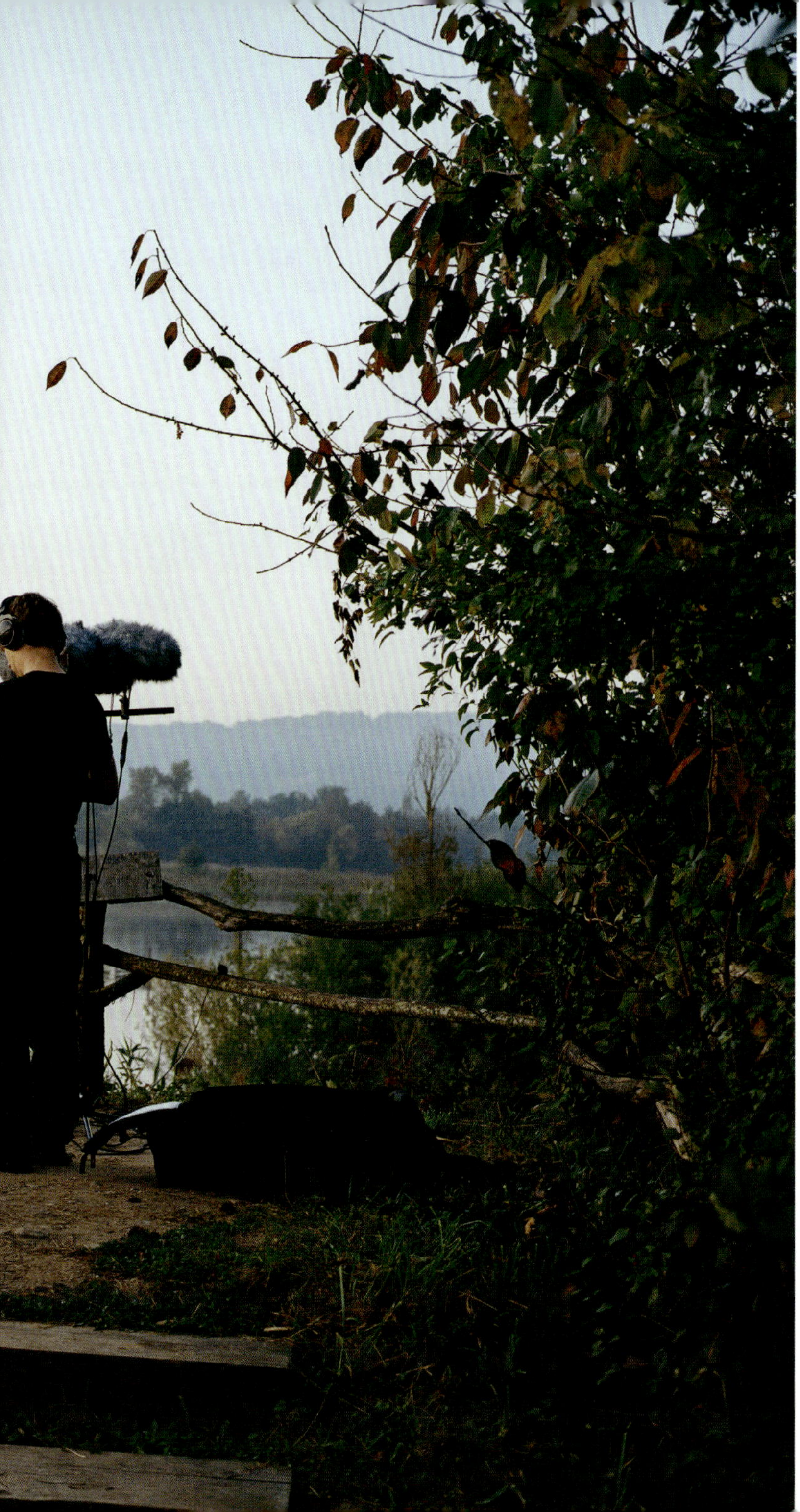

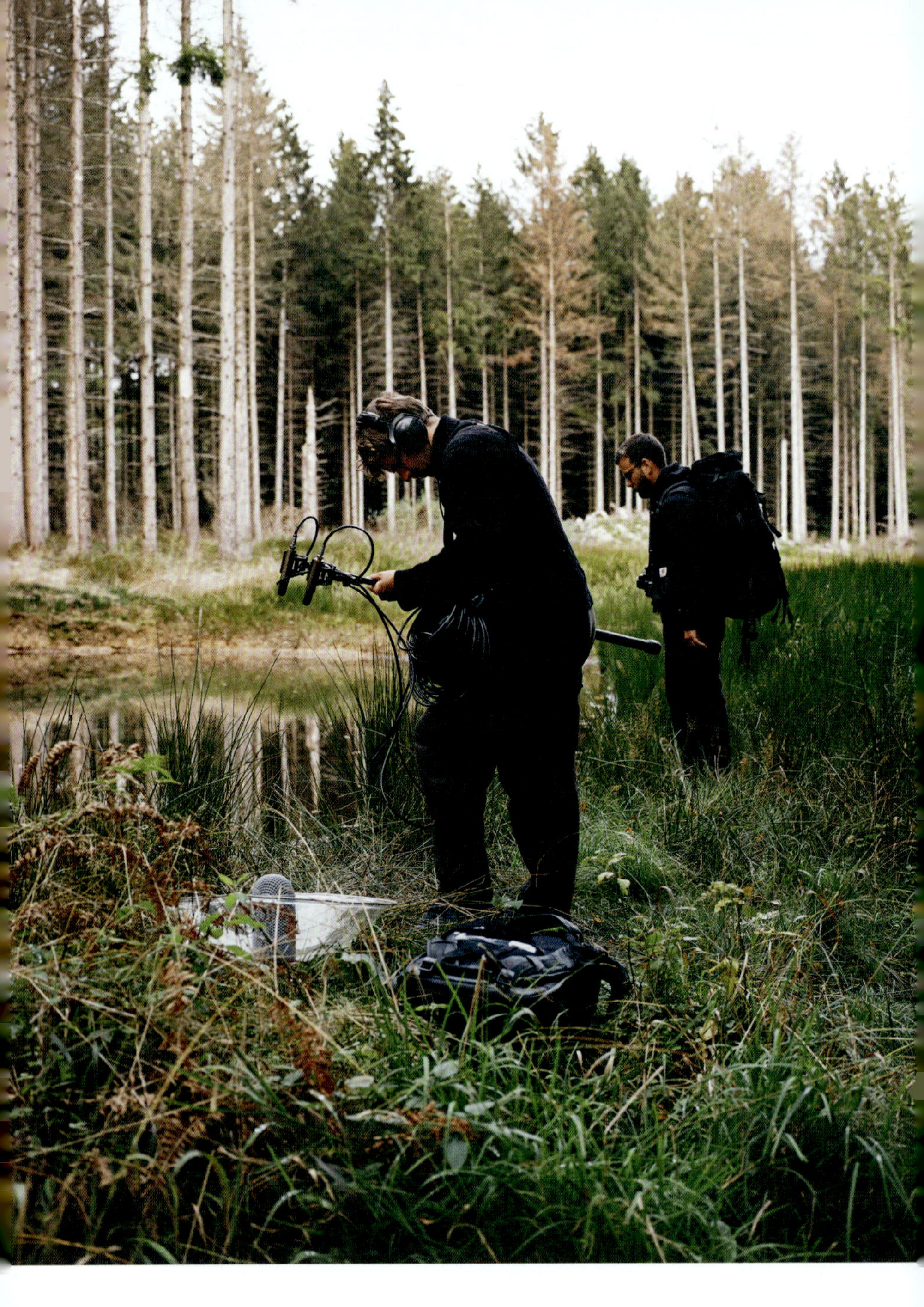

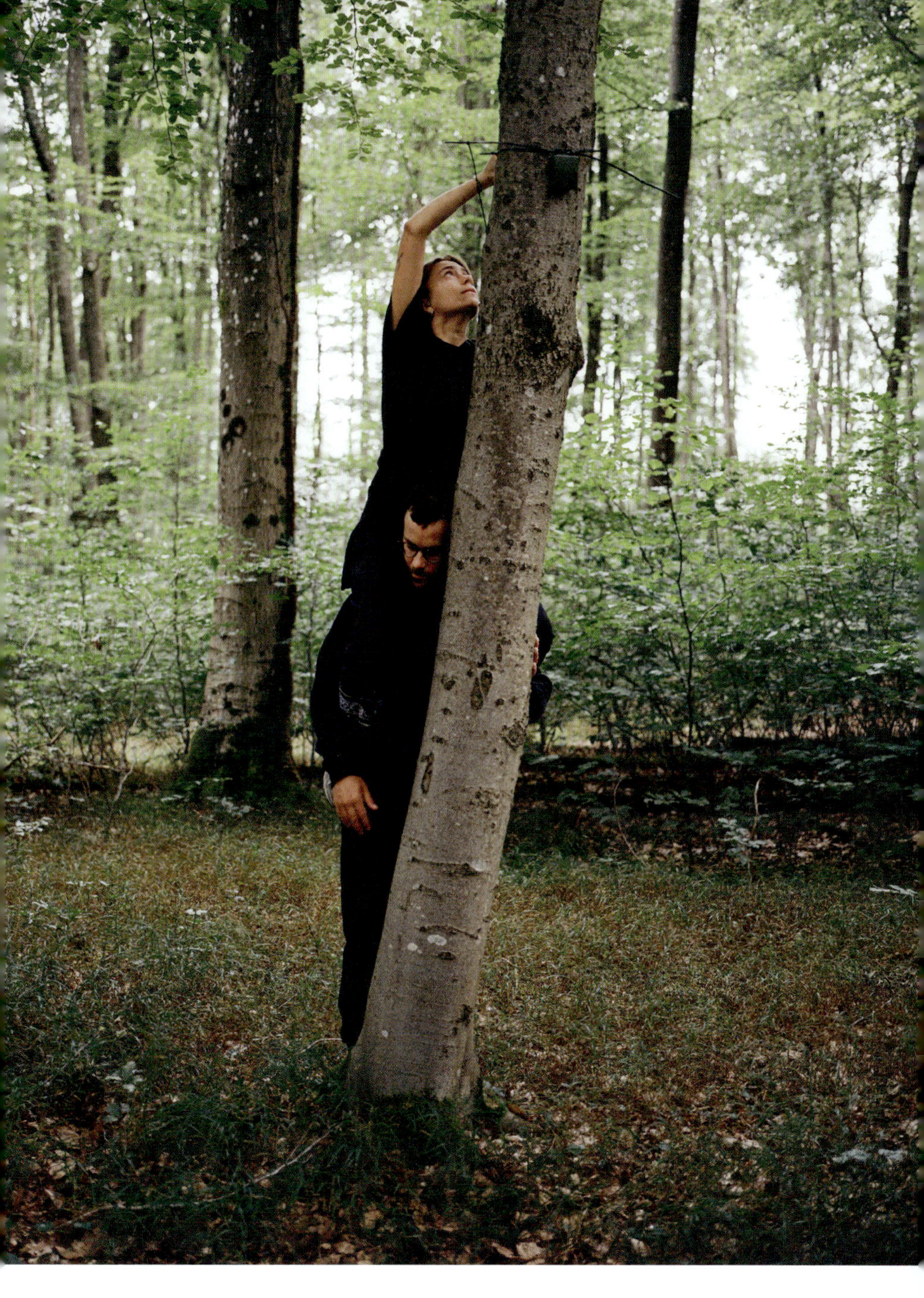

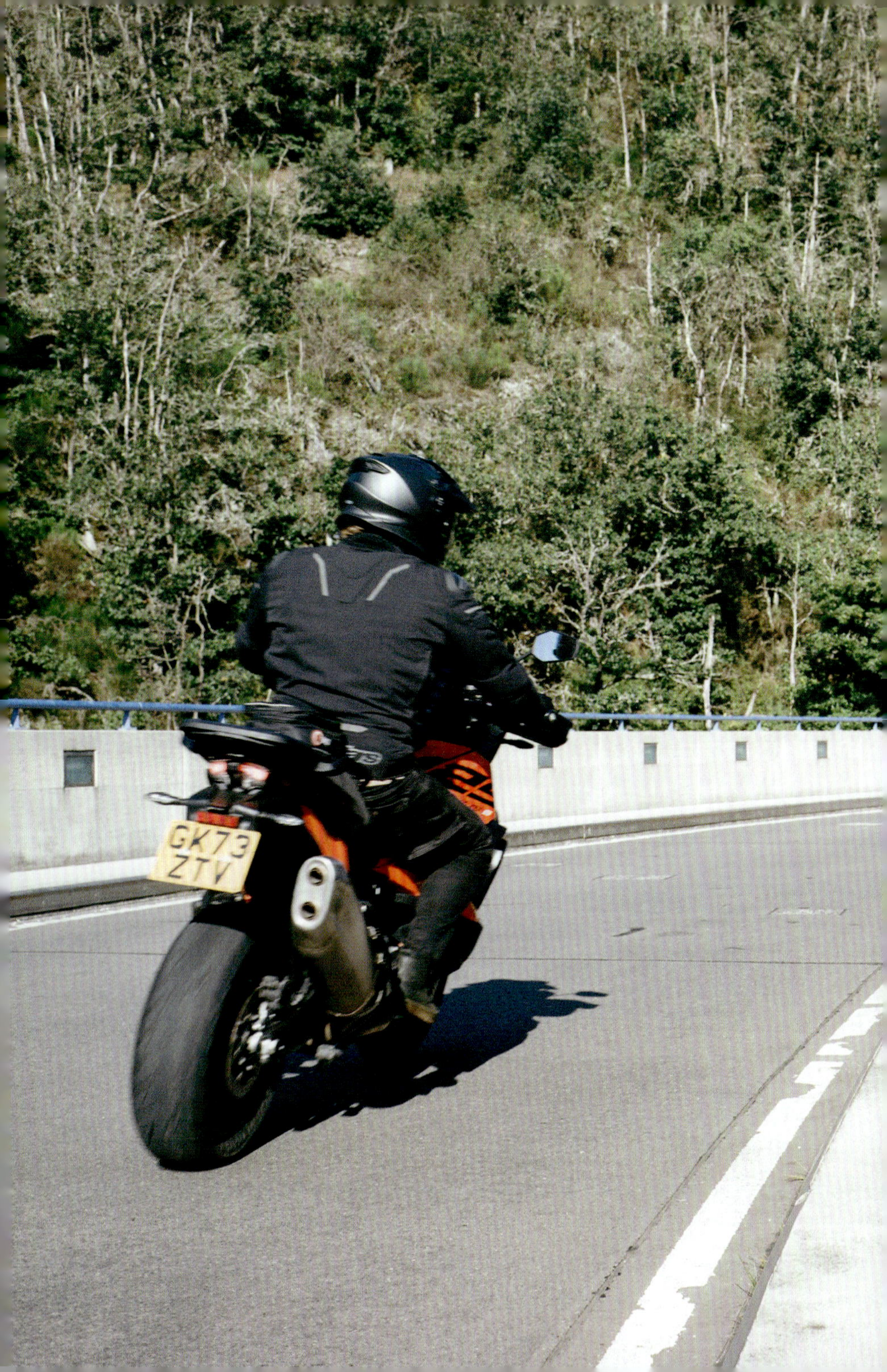
GK73
ZTV

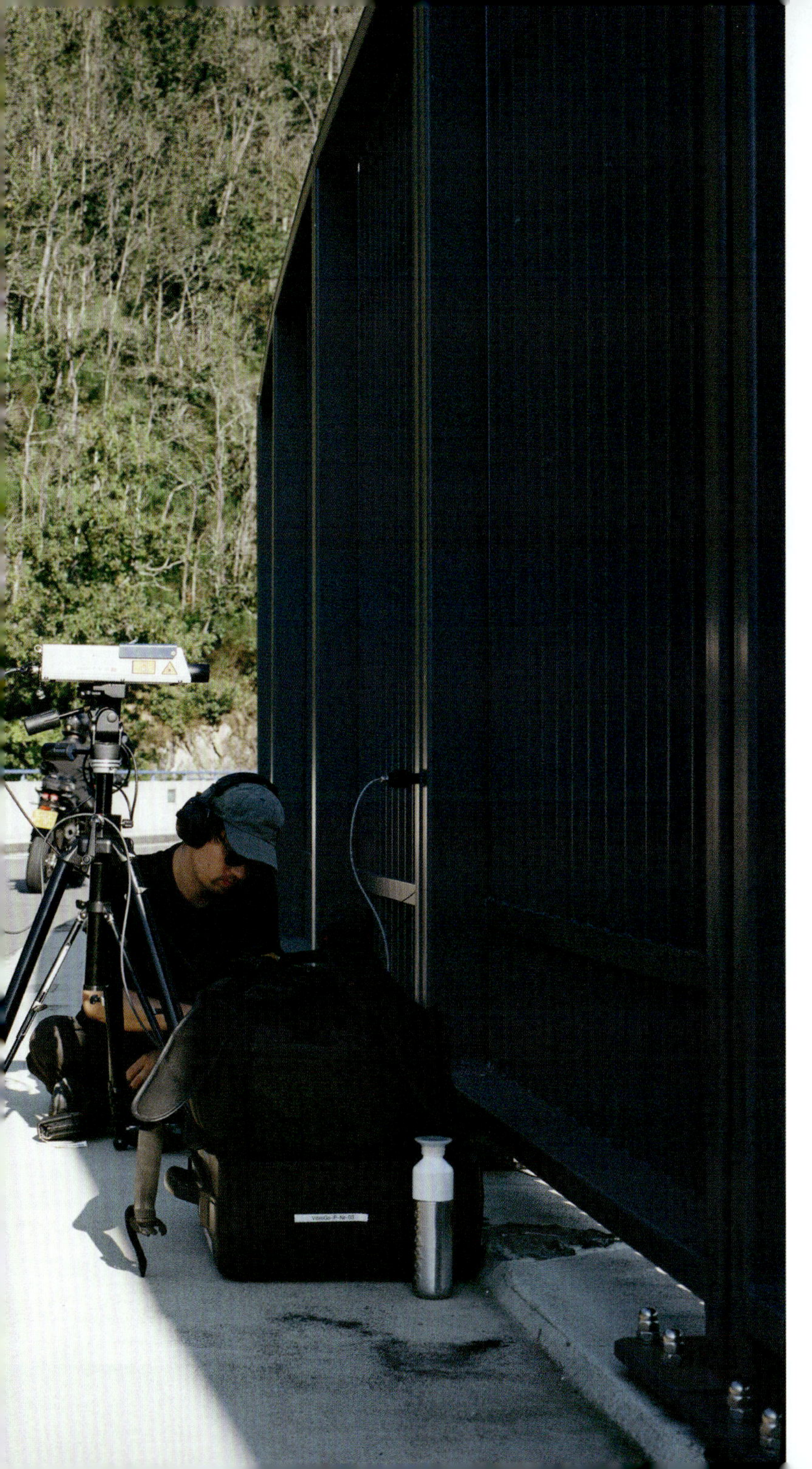

= SPOT 4 _ LIEFRANGE DAM, UP STREAM FROM ESCH-SUR-SÛRE _ SMALLER DAM (OPEN & SMA THE WATER IS BLACK. IT DOESN'T MAKE ELECTI THE DAM ONLY HOLDS THE WATER / QUIETS IT DOWN

- WEATHER = BEAUTIFUL END OF DAY LIGHT AUTUMNY COLORS BEGIN TO APPEAR ON THE LEAV

- EQUIP _ HYDROPHONE

- WORDS = SOUNDS = MUDDY / SOFT / BUBBLE / GENERAL = CALM / CUTE / BLACK /

SUNDAY 22 SEPTEMBRE 2024

- DRIVE TO 2nd HOUSE IN USELDANGE, A LITTLE VILLAGE, CENTER OF THE COUNTRY WITH A CUTE RIVE FLOWING INTO BISSEN (WHERE THE DATA CENTER IS

- EQUIP _ 8 CHANNEL INSTALLATION IN / AROUND THE THE WATER SHORE

WORDS = SOUNDS = FLOWING / AQUATIC / HOLLOW / ONDULATI GENERAL = PEACEFUL / SLIPPERY / RELAXING

STOP IN QUATRE VENTS TO LISTEN TO COOL ANTENNAS. LIKE ANTENNES-RELAIS IN THE BACK OF GARAGE/ AGRI. FARM... NOT SO IMPRESSIVE THE SOUNDS.. WE CONTINUE. (ESCHDORF)

- STOP AT A WIND TURBINE ON THE WAY TO VIANDEN / BETWEEN HEIDERSCHEID & TODLERMÜHLEN EVONOS TURBINE. ES-WK-002.

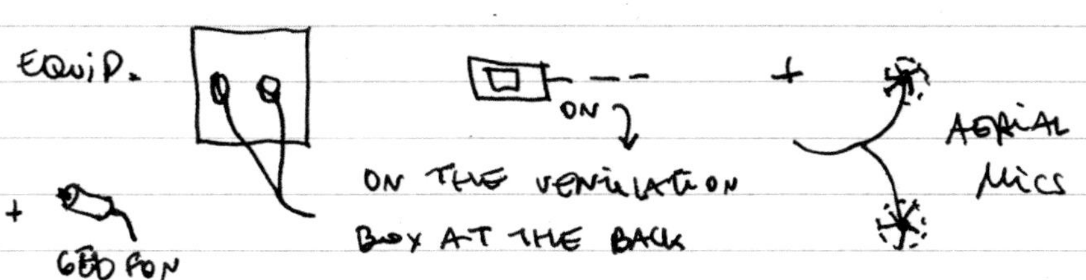

WEATHER IS WARM AND CLOUDY, QUITE SUNNY, OPEN FIELD, CLOSE TO A ROAD BUT NOT SO LOUD, NOT MANY CARS ON A SUNDAY NOON. MANY WIND TURBINES ALL AROUND, EVERYWHERE YOU LOOK THERE IS ONE PLANTED ON TOP ON A HILL (VERY DUTCH LANSCAPE ⊖ THE WATER)

WORDS. SOUNDS = GESTURE / WHISPER / EXHAUST / ROTARY
GENERAL = PLATEAU / FIELD / HILLY / HORIZONTAL

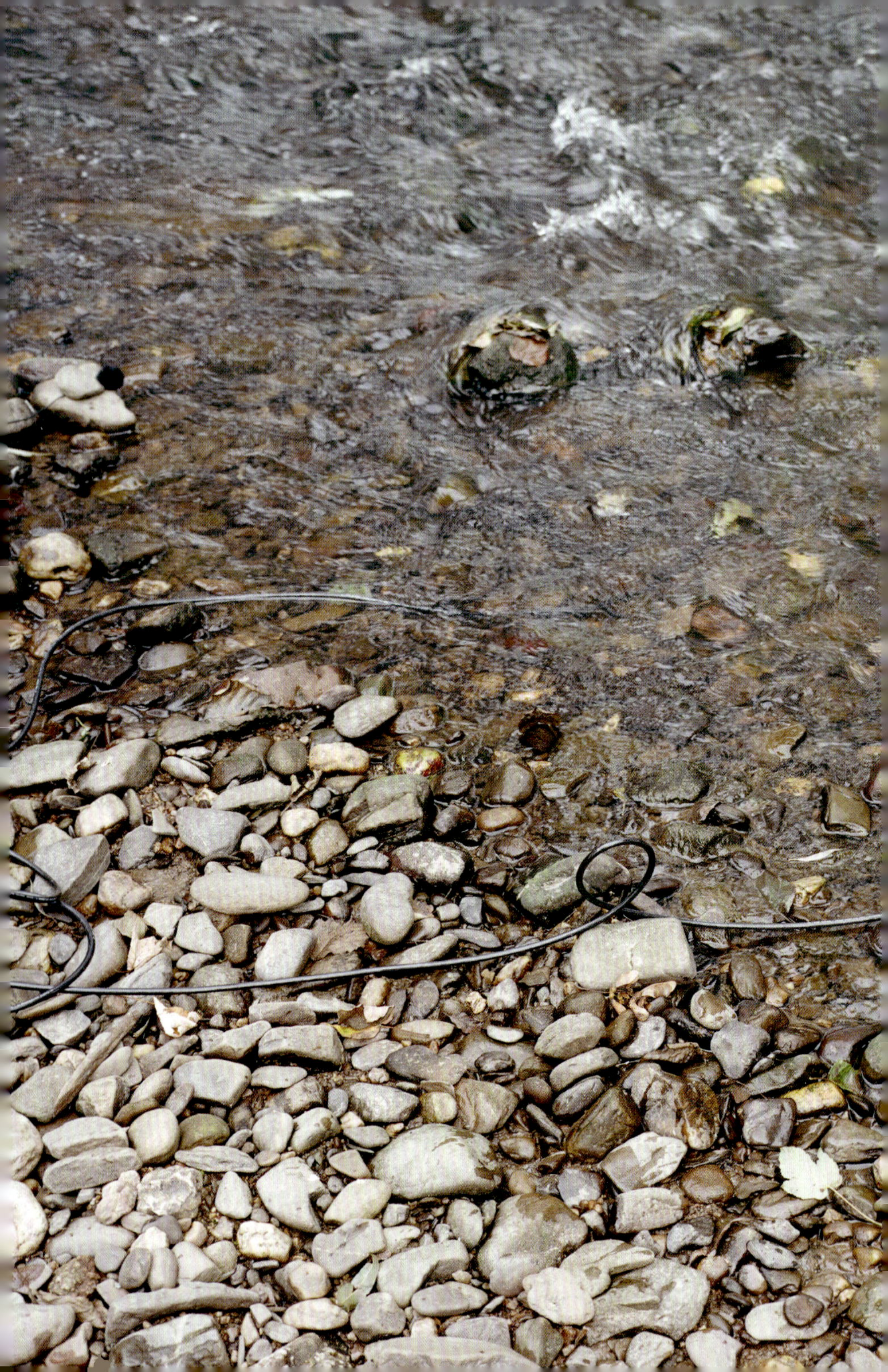

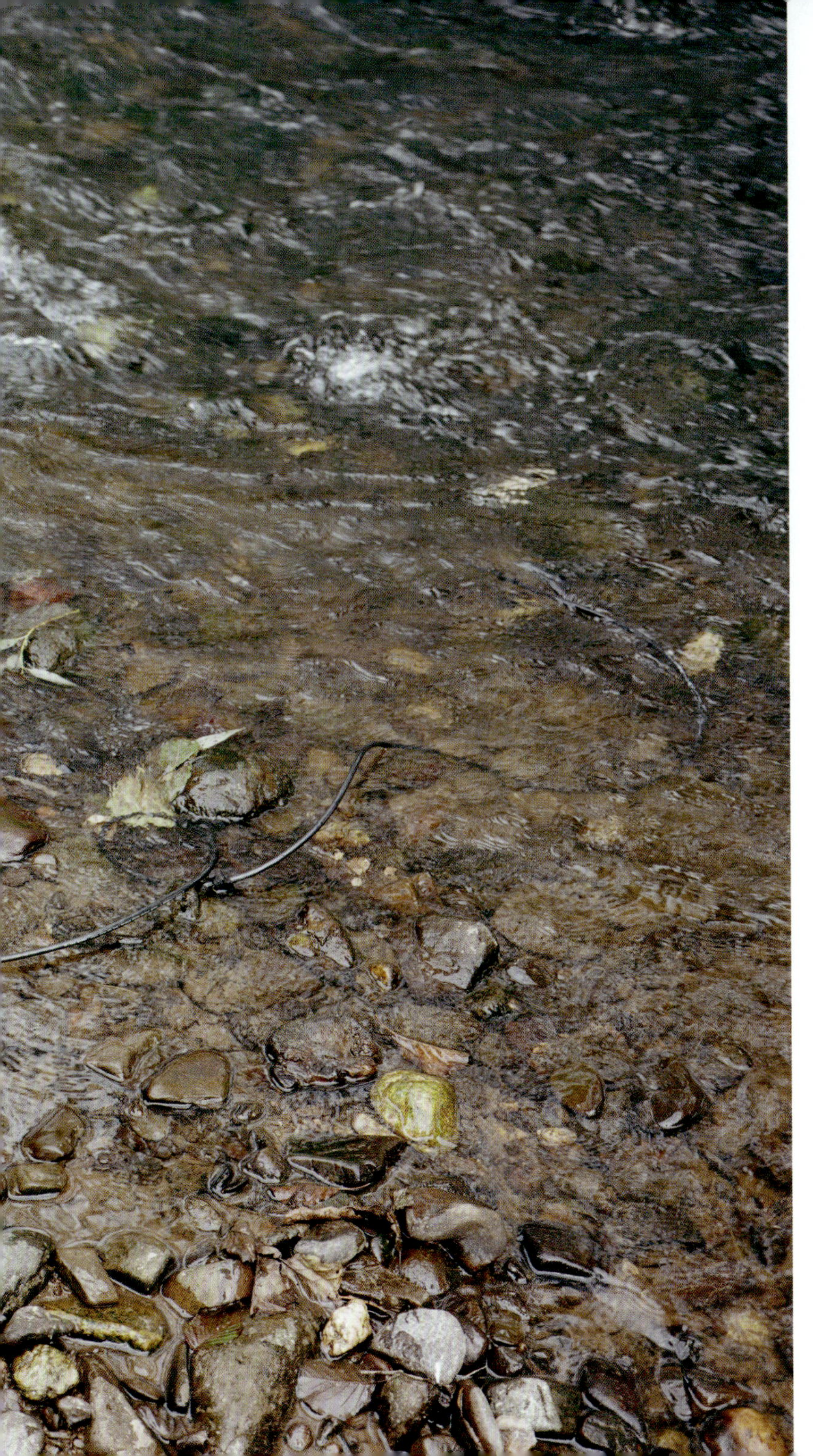

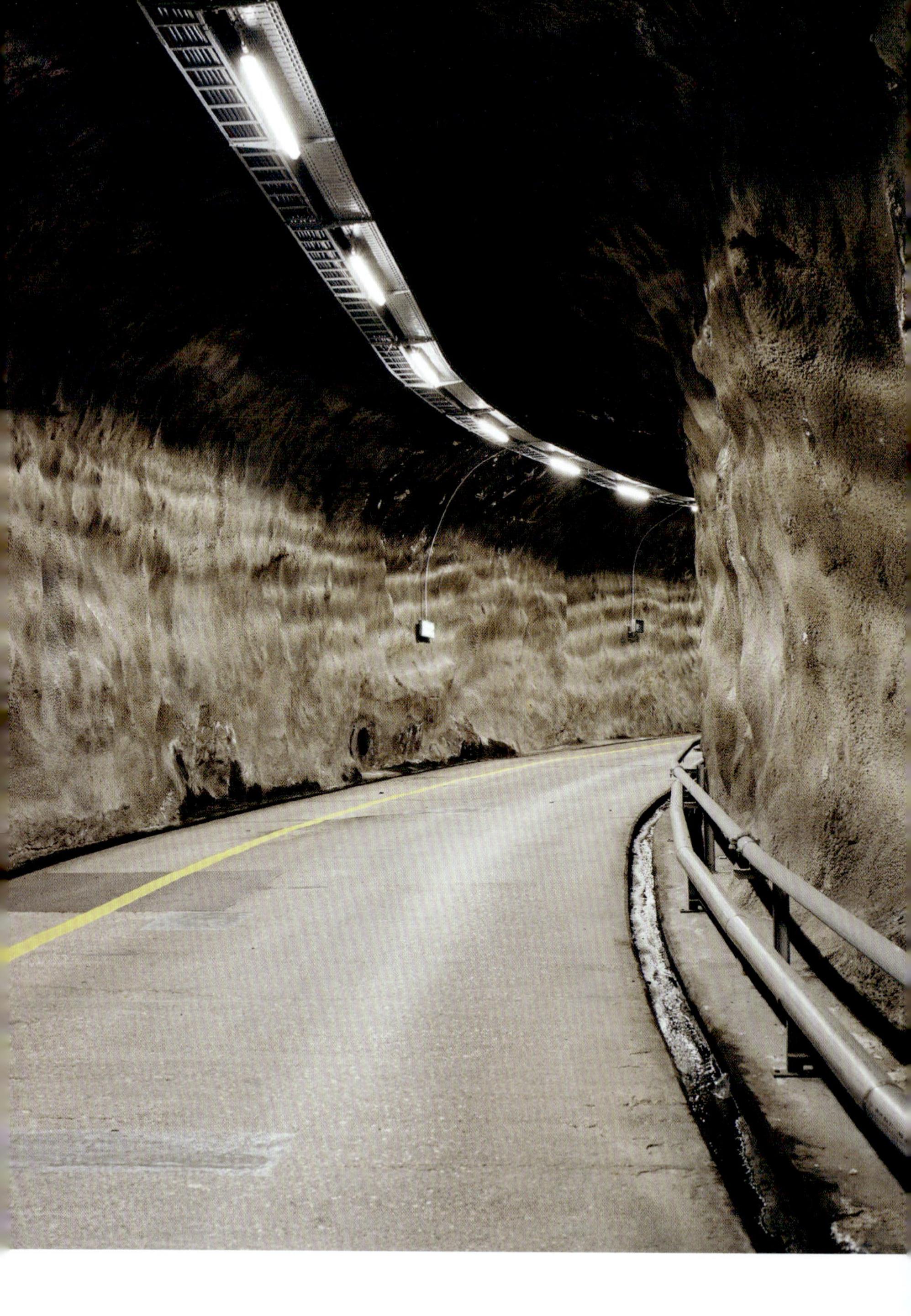

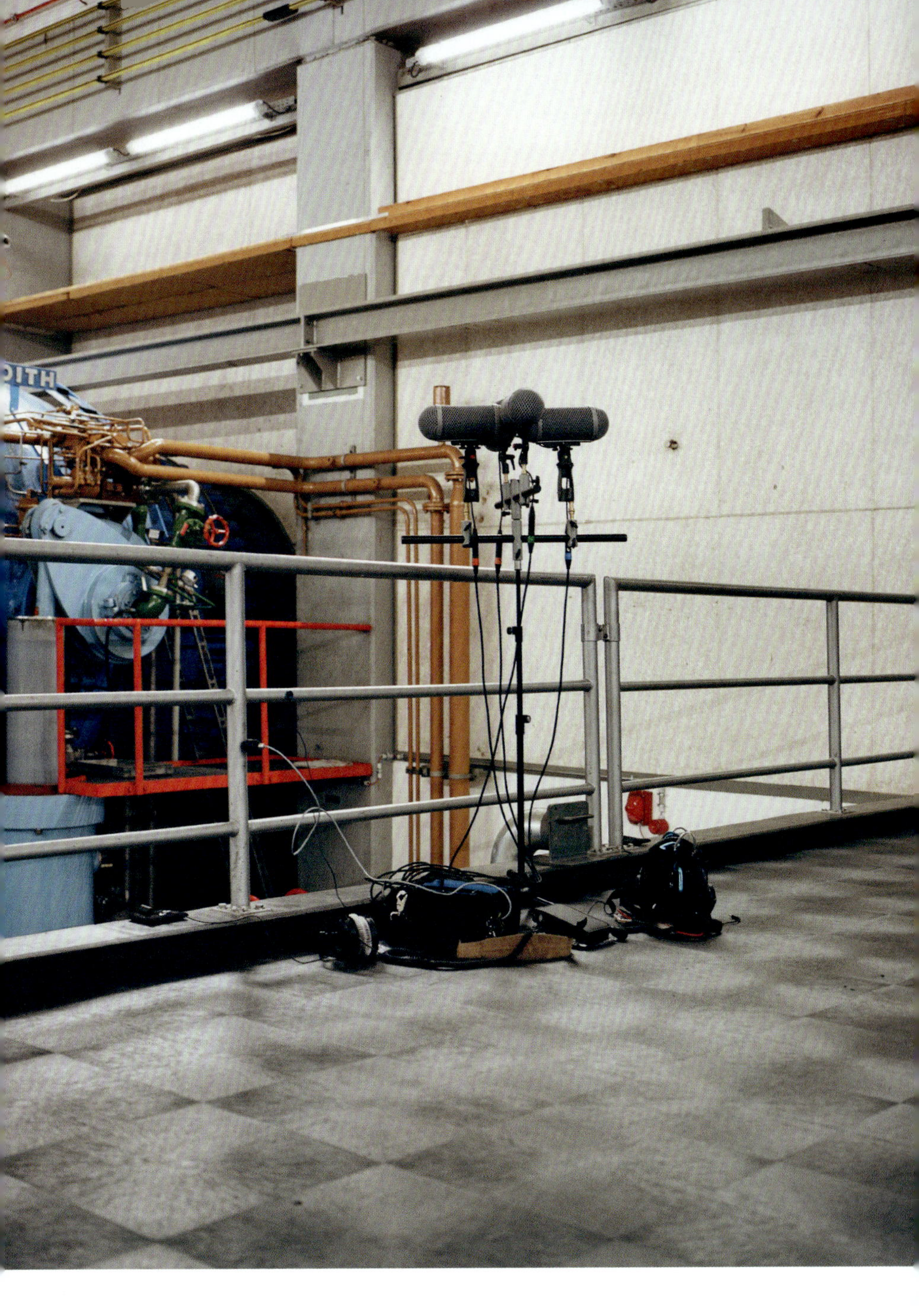

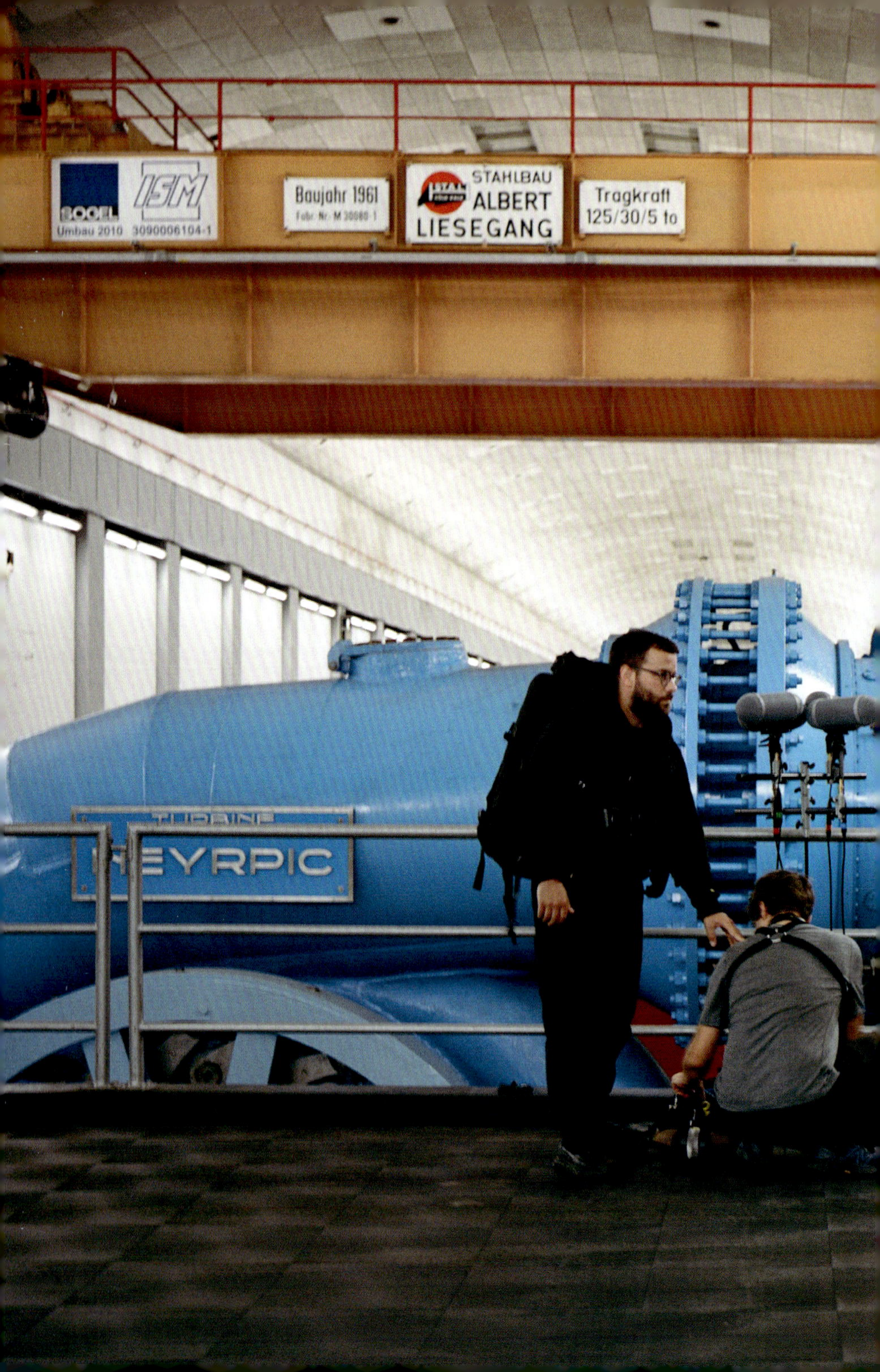
ISM
Umbau 2010
3090006104-1
Baujahr 1961
STAHLBAU
ALBERT
LIESEGANG
Tragkraft
125/30/5 to
TURBINE
EYRPIC

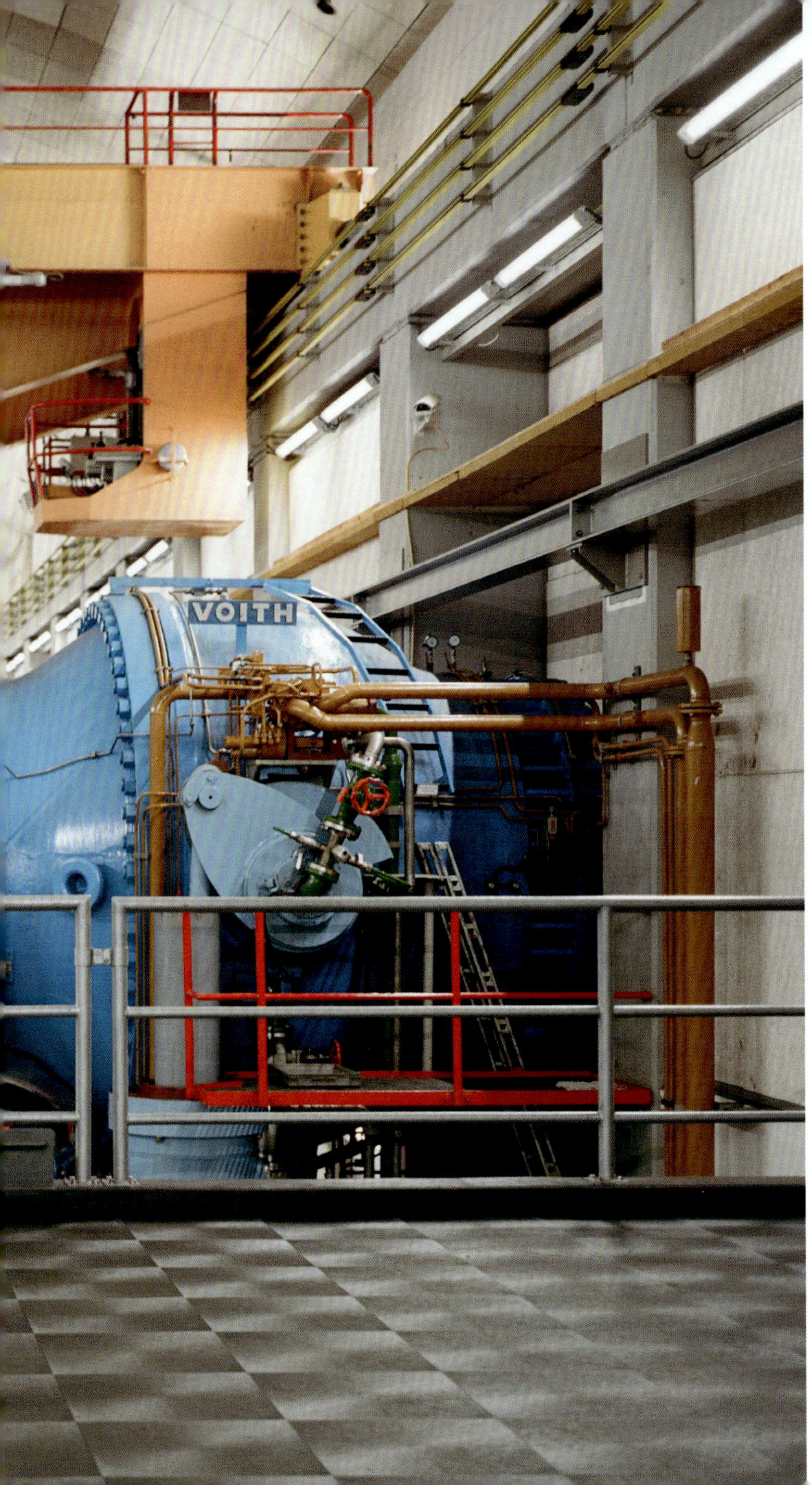
VOITH

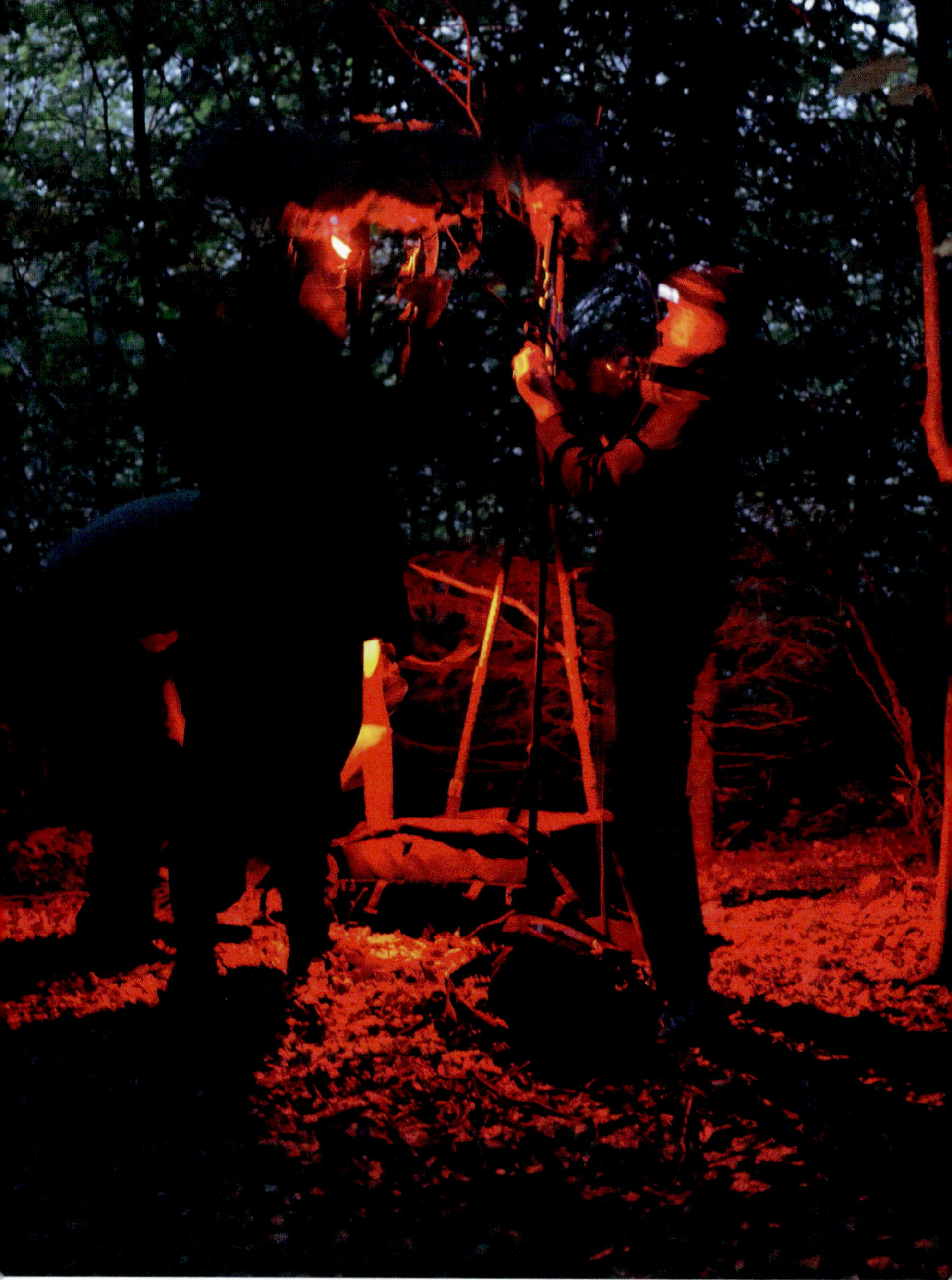

Listening to Infrastructures

Shannon Mattern

The following textual medley proposes listening as a methodology for engaging with and intervening within urban systems, natural ecologies, and their zones of intersection. The first text, originally published in 2021, suggests what we might learn by listening across the scales of logistical networks—from individual laboring bodies and machines, to docks and warehouses, to sublime global systems. The second text, originally published in 2013, sonifies the meso scale: bridges and wires and other infrastructural installations. Listening here attunes us to their rhythms and operative logics. The third and final text, originally published in 2020, explores urban auscultation—both immediate and "acoustic," and mediated through mechanical and digital instruments. We consider what harmonies might exist between the embodied practices of intimate medical auscultation and the clinical pattern recognition executed by cyborgian ears sensing at the metropolitan scale.

[From "The Pulse of Global Passage"]

Logistics, as a "deeply incoherent, contradictory, conflicted, and competitive domain," Alberto Toscano explains, possesses a "fundamental opacity."[1]

That opacity presents an opportunity for another mode of representation and investigation: listening. Logistical systems are assemblages of maps and surveillance footage and customs forms, but they're also symphonies of beeps and shouts and fog horns. Listening has long been central to logical operations, and sounding media—from booming canons to voices to RFID [Radio Frequency Identification] tags—have long regimented its operations. . . . Listening to infrastructures can help us understand their mechanisms and rhythms of operation, as well as how their broader spatial contexts function as sites of sonic communication. Logistics *is* a rhythm; it's an orchestration of infrastructures to facilitate movement, a means of synchronizing disparate temporalities. And sound is well qualified to mark those rhythms, register logistics' political and cultural dynamics, sound out its environments of operation, and capture its affective dimensions. . . .

. . . Logistics both compels and conditions various modes of listening. Diagnostic, orientational, and defensive listening enable dock-workers, deckhands, soldiers, and factory and maintenance workers to appraise the proper functioning of the system; to coordinate actions (both compliant and disruptive); to assess their own safety; and, if necessary, to get out of harm's way. Ethical and critical listening can help us to tune into the system's power dynamics and to recognize, even empathize, with other logistical subjects, including those on the other end of the supply chain. While it might seem that critical listening would benefit from an outsider's perspective, we'll come to see that it, like all others modes of listening, can take place from anywhere: on the dock, in the fields, or at the supermarket. Listening-as-method is particularly well suited for thinking across logistics' scales of operation, attuned to the resonances between the micro and macro.[2] We can lend an ear to local operations and attend to individual logistical agents, while also listening from a remove—across space and time, through abstraction or speculation—to sound out big patterns and macro-scale rhythms. We can extrapolate from the sonic qualities of particular logistical nodes—from the cacophony of the battlefield to a quiet respite at the bow of a container ship—to index the flows of goods and capital, bodies and affect, throughout the system. Logistics also offers up countless sonic stimuli for our consideration: languages, both natural and artificial; environmental sounds; objects' resonances; electronic signals; and machinic rhythms. Such a crowded acoustic field has made it increasingly necessary for us to supplement our own ears with machinic sensors and algorithmic processors, creating cyborgian listening subjects.

All this is to say: listening to logistics attunes us to new dimensions and dynamics of logistical systems past and present, *and* it enables us to think anew about what it means to listen in an age of global capitalism and automation. . . .

. . . Even well before the rise of a "business science" of logistics, sounds played a crucial role in the movement of goods and people. Elevated voices were once the means by which dockworkers secured work. In 1857, Henry Mayhew described the "scuffling and scrambling, and stretching forth of countless hands high in the air, to catch the eye of him whose nod can give them work. . . . All are shouting; some cry aloud his surname, and some his Christian name; and some call out their own names, to remind him that they are there."[3] Those same voices were then deployed during long shifts to ensure the efficient movement of goods, equipment, and bodies. Managers shouted orders, and longshoremen called out verbal cues to one another. In more recent years, those voices have extended their reach via VHF maritime mobile band radio. Radio connects agents on dock, on deck, in cranes perched high above the action, and in vessel traffic control, all speaking a machinic patois that maximizes efficiency and intelligibility. Today, as yesterday, bells, whistles, horns, and alarms are part of the mix, too, warning of the comings and goings of ships and equipment, both close and distant. Listening on the docks has long been a means of recognition, logistical coordination, and self-defense.

The equipment itself makes quite a racket. Yet that racket contains useful information and thus requires close listening. According to a recent report from a team of occupational health researchers, a fifty-five-year-old dockworker

> reported exposure to frequent impact noise from metal striking metal. He noted that, when operating the crane, he had to shout to be able to communicate to a co-worker nearby. He did not wear hearing protection, saying that he needed to hear sounds (such as that of the overhead crane when he was loading), and to shout communication when he we operating the crane. For 1 or 2 hours a day, he operated a forklift in a refrigerated warehouse, where noise from the refrigeration units was so loud that he had to shout to communicate with a co-worker at arm's length. He did not wear hearing protection when he drove the forklift because of the need to hear warning signals and communication from co-workers.[4]

Not surprisingly, all that close listening causes hearing loss. . . .

Cacophony is a sonic index of a busy port, of readily circulating goods and laboring bodies, of a strong global economy.[5] In other words, what's bad for dockworkers' eardrums is ultimately good for business. As ethnographer Charmaine Chua explains, "A quiet port is logistics' nightmare."[6] And there are countless forces that have the power to silence particular nodes within the supply chain: from labor disputes to truck shortages to ports' failure to "scale-up" in order to accommodate ever-bigger ships. Chua explains that local snafus can easily become global: "Built on precisely-timed coordination between shippers and suppliers, the system is so vulnerable that what might have been a minor shock in the past today produces a domino effect that has worldwide echoes." Her sonic metaphor hints at an acoustic methodology: we can use the quiet port as a diagnostic for disruption within the broader logistical system. Local silence can signal global discord. . . .

The ship in transit inhabits another acoustic environment. The sea, John Durham Peters suggests, is "a natural laboratory for altered sense rations," and Chua has written eloquently about her own sensory experience of riding the supply chain aboard a container ship from Los Angeles to Taipei.[7] I quote Chua at length:

> The bow of the ship is the only place . . . that affords a modicum of silence. To get there, you walk down the length of the narrow grey deck, flanked on one side by containers crowded into towering stacks that scrape and creak against each other as the ship cuts through the waves, and on the other by the powerful sweep of a wind so strong that you have to fight not to be blown backwards. At the foremost tip of the ship, you climb a few steps onto a large open deck . . . and suddenly, the mechanical roar of the ship falls away. . . . [From there,] you can look outward onto an endless, unbroken horizon of ocean in near quiet, and almost think that the ship is barely moving.[8]

This romantic image of escape—which is kind of the open-sea version of wearing noise-canceling headphones in an open-plan office reminds us again that there are pockets of restorative silence within this cacophonous system; that the human laborer, in an act of self-preservation, must occasionally unplug from the logistical system, turn down the volume. . . .

. . . Logistics' "entire network of infrastructures, technologies, spaces, [and] workers," Cowen says, "remains tucked out of sight" for most of us.[9] It remains mostly inaudible too: we rarely hear the whirr of conveyor belts, the roar of the refrigeration units, or the stifled sobs of the cooks and engine crew. And we can't discern, from amidst the distant roar of overhead jets, which might emanate from the FedEx 777 delivering our Amazon Prime order (though there has been much romanticization of certain logistical sounds—particularly the distant train whistle and foghorn). . . .

Before they're deposited at our doorstep—by truck, by pushcart, or, perhaps soon, by drone—those packages are cycled through a distribution center. Unlike a traditional warehouse, where things are stored, the distribution center sorts and redirects; it "keeps stuff in motion."[10] Again, sounding technologies help to orchestrate that movement. While the trucks, trains, robots, products, and people circulating through and around these centers are tracked via radio frequency identification tags, the distribution center's workers, or "pickers," are guided by voice-picking software.[11] As Jesse LeCavalier explains, "A synthesized [female] voice directs the worker to different locations in the distribution center, prompting him or her to pick certain quantities of particular items. The worker then vocally confirms the completion of each task."[12] Listening is a means of orientation and synchronization.

Because our workers are focused on close listening to the super-fast-talking automated voice, they're unable to use their *own* voices to communicate with others—anyone other than the computer, that is. With no time wasted on socialization, pickers can maximize their performance. A worker can ask the machine, "How am I doing?" and the software will deliver a progress report. And because the system can be programmed to speak in workers' native languages, LeCavalier says, "It demonstrates a greater capacity for communication with workers than many human managers."[13] As a company spokesperson told LeCavalier, it's "like having a supervisor stand over your shoulder."[14] It's a means of disciplining the ears and, by extension, the body, in order to "integrate workers into the system and calibrate the rhythms of their movements with the needs of an automated system of stuff," Cowen proposes.[15] And then, at the consumer end of the supply chain, at the grocery store checkout, a coda: the barcode beep, that human-intelligible sound of global trade reduced to a micro-scale, machine-readable graphic. Listening offers confirmation that we're doing our jobs, as pickers and consumers, properly. . . .

What else might we learn about logistics by listening from a distance, algorithmically? Some cities deploy networked sound sensors at distributed locations to assess noise pollution, much of which is caused by logistical systems. City officials correlate those noise readings with data about road surfaces, vehicle counts, traffic speed, topology, and other variables, then create daytime and nighttime sound maps that help managers make decisions about noise reduction policies. Here, Claudio Coletta and Rob Kitchin proclaim, "We have a set of algo-rhythms at work, algorithmically measuring, processing, and analyzing urban sound and its rhythms."[16] John Mannes reports that several companies are developing systems to automate the sonic monitoring of mechanical systems–railways, oil drills, power plants, and so forth. Some players in this field are building training sets with sound samples of well-behaved machines, while others listen across a vast array of systems, identify anomalies, and invite engineers and other experts in to help them analyze and classify those aberrant sounds.[17] . . .

Sound, [artist-researcher Wesley] Goatley told me, is well suited to disabuse us of our delusions of omniscience and aspirations to see the world through a "conquering gaze from nowhere."[18] As Donna Haraway proposes, "We must be hostile to easy . . . holisms built out of summing and subsuming parts," much like those totalizing logistical maps and black boxed logistical software systems. Instead, we should aspire to a "self critical partiality" that allows us to imagine "worlds less organized by axes of domination"—worlds in which, perhaps, we can hear the Filipino seamen's laments, or the deafened blue whale swimming aimlessly below the ship, or the unemployed dockworker in a quiet port city.[19] Sound, Goatley says, "offers both a form of sensing larger rhythms, repetitions, and patterns in space in an embodied fashion distinct from the visual," and it also allows for an intimate engagement with these systems.[20]

... Listening across logistics' scales helps us to orient ourselves within its interlocking systems: to feel the rhythms of its local nodes, to recognize and give voice to its local agents, to re-sound its ambient environments and, at the same time, to extrapolate from the micro-scale in order to imagine the orchestration of goods and capital and bodies throughout the system, to hear the pulses of global passage. This "telephoning" out, expanding the scale of attunement (more often, now, with the aid of algorithmic ears), allows us to sound out bigger patterns—cacophonies and silences, harmonies and discord—in global capitalism. By rendering logistics *sense*-able, listening-as-method proposes new epistemological frameworks for what we can know about logistics' silenced pasts and encrypted data, and how we sonically register its operations through logistical media. Listening can supplement our other means of logistical mediation—like maps and flowcharts and photographs of shipping containers—to offer new tools of ethical investment and political critique.

[From "Ear to the Wire"]

What tools might we use to explore these material assemblages—or, to use a hackneyed phrase, "make visible the invisible" infrastructures—that power urban life? What if we took media and network archaeology *literally*, and borrowed a few tricks from archaeologists of the Indiana Jones ... variety? What if we picked up their trowels and surveying tools? ...

... Material infrastructures constitute a layered landscape that lends itself to *digging into*; they leave material residues that we can dig up. For instance, historical communication networks offer artifacts like pneumatic tubes, telegraph cables, structures for postal delivery, technologies for the production and dissemination of early print forms, palimpsests of writing on city walls. But what of those communication systems composed of few objects you can either hit with a shovel or unearth in an archive? How does one *dig into* a form of mediation that seemingly *has* no physical form? Consider the "sonic city"—the city of radio waves and public address and everyday conversation. Its "artifacts" are primarily ephemeral; their echoes have long since faded. Yet the material spaces in which those echoes once reverberated can offer invaluable clues about how cities (re-)sound. We can draw on the work of archaeologists-proper (and, ideally, collaborate with them) to learn about our media networks by excavating their urban contexts. Archaeology and its subfield of archaeoacoustics, along with architectural and urban history and allied fields, can help us to understand the ways in which radio and sound waves have interacted with, and even shaped, the material city—how our urban surfaces, volumes, and voids have functioned as sounding boards, resonance chambers, and transmission media. What we'll ultimately find is that our media histories are deeply "networked" with our urban and architectural histories, and that, in many cases, these cultural and technological forms are mutually constructed. As we head into a future in which, on the one hand, we face an unpredictably evolving acoustic ecology, and, on the other, we have greater potential to "sound-design" or acoustically engineer our cities, appreciating the entanglement of these histories will help us to move forward in a more critical fashion....

... In recent years, archaeologists have begun to pay more attention to acoustics—from the sounds produced in ancient sites by historical musical instruments or tools, to the acoustic properties of various locations, and how they informed drama, everyday speech, or a variety of other performative and communicative activities. Archaeologists working in the field of *archaeoacoustics* have studied the sonic architectures of various ancient sites, from Stonehenge to Peruvian temples to American petroglyph sites, wondering how acoustics might have informed ritual performance and oration, as well as inhabitants' experiences. Of course there's much conjecture involved in piecing together ancient multisensory experiences and ancient builders' intentionality, and the speculative nature of such archaeoacoustics research has generated debate.[21] . . .

[In modern history,] new telecommunications technologies gave rise to new infrastructural elements—electricity poles, cables, antennas, transmission towers—that transformed both urban and rural landscapes.[22] Urban historians and historians of technology who focus on the telephone in particular seem to have come to the conclusion that it had both centripetal and centrifugal influences on urbanization. It allowed businesses to concentrate their offices downtown, while relocating their factories, warehouses, and shipping facilities outside the city, and it freed city residents to move out to the end of the streetcar lines with reassurance that the news and activity of the city was only a phone call away.[23]

Architectural historian Carlotta Daro argues that those wires profoundly informed how designers shaped the landscape: "professional practice of telecommunications engineering was absorbed by modernist architects and urban planners and synthesized as a new kind of technological vision of both town and country." Lewis Mumford represented one such group of planners: the Regional Planning Association of America. In 1937, he wrote in *Architectural Record*: "The area of potential urban settlement has been vastly increased by the motor car and the airplane; but, the necessity for solid contiguous growth, for the purposes of the intercourse, has in turn been lessened by the telephone and the radio."[24] These new, liberating technologies—what he called *neotechnics*—have afforded planners an opportunity to consider alternatives to increasing urban concentration. And he, and the RPAA, of which he was a co-founder and spokesperson, advocated instead for *planned* decentralization.

[From "Urban Auscultation"]

Many of the modern technologies used to sound out the city are inspired by diagnostic tools from medicine and psychology. Through these soundings, we grasp the city's internal mechanics, assess the materiality of its parts, analyze its rhythms.[25] And those two domains, surveillance and health, are increasingly entwined with a third, machine intelligence.[26]

With all the attention given to urban applications of machine vision—from facial recognition systems to autonomous vehicles—it's easy to forget about machines that *listen* to the city. Google scientist Dan Ellis has called machine listening a "poor second" to machine vision; there's not as much research dedicated to machine listening, and it's frequently reduced to speech recognition.[27] Yet we can learn a lot about urban processes and epistemologies by studying how machines listen to cities; or, rather, how humans use machines to listen to cities. . . .

How we imagine ourselves as listening subjects, as hearing bodies, informs how we make sense of our sonic environments. As we listen to the city with both human and machinic ears, we sound it out as a particular kind of resonant or reflective body or system. If we are constantly listening for alien accents or breaking glass and gunfire—as some automated police systems do—we might imagine the city as a body that needs protection from threats. If our stock-trading bots equate the hum of vehicular traffic with economic production, we might be alarmed by quiet streets. If, instead, we listen to the city at macro scale, as an ecology of diverse lifeforms and resources and habitats, we might recognize a dynamic, vital system to be stewarded for future generations of humans and other species. . . . Our tools for urban listening embody particular ways of knowing the city, with implications for how the city is designed, administered, policed, beautified, and maintained.

In other words, *how* we listen to the city is as important as what we are listening for. Amid the rise of artificially intelligent, algorithmically attuned ears, scoring the city in accordance with their own computational logics, we humans need to better understand our own acoustic agency so that we can make thoughtful choices about how to supplement our ears with machinic ones. In a world defined by climate crisis, surveillance capitalism, and the periodic collapse of global health, we need to think as much about a city's *resonance* as we do about its resilience and livability. . . .

. . . In 1906, Julia Barnett Rice, a non-practicing medical doctor, founded New York's Society for the Suppression of Unnecessary Noise, which lobbied for quiet zones around city hospitals and national legislation like the Bennet Act, which regulated boat whistles in urban harbors.[28] Soon afterward, philosopher Theodor Lessing founded the German Association for the Protection from Noise, which convinced some cities to install noise-dampening pavements and regulate train signals and steam hammers.[29]

And the new urban administrative machine required new tools to regulate the machinic environment. The portable audiometer produced a "subjective" measure of loudness; its operator compared a test sound with a reference tone, which could be dialed down until it was masked by the sound under investigation. A later technology, the acoustimeter, added a microphone, amplifier, and indicator signal, eliminating the need for user judgment. These new tools of urban auscultation were combined with a new unit of measurement, the decibel, to produce the first urban noise surveys in London, New York, Chicago, and Washington, D.C., in the 1920s. As Karin Bijsterveld notes, "Although audiometers were at first used in a strictly medical context to test hearing, the city turned out to be a crucial context for [their] development and application."[30]

This context quickly revealed the limits of efforts to instrumentalize and objectify hearing. The meters couldn't replicate the way human ears perceived loudness, and they had trouble tracking fluctuating sounds. Bell Labs' Rogers Galt, who reviewed urban sound surveys for the *Journal of the Acoustical Society of America* in 1930, emphasized the subjective, situational nature of aural perception. Whether a sound was perceived as noise, he wrote, depended on how long it lasted and how often it occurred, whether it was steady or intermittent, who made the sound, who was disturbed, and whether the sound was understood as necessary.[31] "Noise" was a product of acoustics and psychology.

Whether or not cities actually were too loud, measurable "noise levels," with their positivist certainty, "became the sign of how bad the situation was."[32] Public health concerns were taken seriously only after noise exposure could be quantified. Leonardo Cardoso, in his study of sound politics in São Paolo, argues that the seemingly objective measurements produced by sound-level meters came to "replac[e] our ears as the authoritative hearing actor" and ultimately conditioned our hearing to a world that the instrument could validate. "Through the minuscule repetition of a series of exposures to sound that are allowed to exist thanks to the [meter's] validation, this technological being" has reshaped our own organic perceptual instruments.[33] We became attuned to what the machine is capable of sensing.

. . . Many cities, including New York, Dublin, Sydney, Paris, and Singapore, have deployed distributed networks of sound sensors to assess urban noise. The Sounds of New York City (SONYC) project, run by NYU's Center for Urban Science and Progress and developed in collaboration with the city departments of health, environmental protection, and parks and recreation, has placed dozens of sensors to "monitor, analyze, and mitigate noise pollution."[34] Each node includes a microphone and a small Raspberry Pi computer, and the data are processed by machine listening—specifically, by artificial intelligence trained on audio datasets annotated by "citizen scientist" volunteers according to a taxonomy of urban sounds. The aim is to extract "meaningful information" from environmental audio, so that cities can identify and target specific sound sources that present problems, like jackhammers, idling engines, loud HVAC, barking dogs, or car horns.[35] . . .

. . . In a city zoned by performance standards, algorithmic auscultation with embedded sensors could be a means of discipline and regulation.[36] As Cardoso foretold, the acoustic panopticon—the panacousticon—would compel human bodies to operate in accordance with its machinic logic.[37]

. . . We can imagine a future city whose acoustic qualities are computationally tuned to promote physical and mental health. (Researchers have already proposed using computer audition to monitor the spread of Covid-19 and ensure social distancing.[38]) Yet data ethicists warn that the racial and gender biases built into our measuring machines will further inequities in care, as they have in medicine and in the provision of urban services like housing and policing.[39]

The turn toward algorithmic city planning mirrors what is happening in medical offices. Some health professionals worry that the stethoscope is going out of fashion, supplanted by echocardiography and handheld ultrasound devices that increase the physical and affective distance between doctor and patient. Yet anthropologist Tom Rice finds that some physicians remain committed to auscultation as an "index of sympathetic and empathetic medical practice."[40] So, too, could we commit ourselves to sounding out the city with more empathic modes of instrumented listening. . . .

Using the example of a car engine, Bijsterveld draws a distinction between "monitory listening," which tells drivers whether the internal mechanisms of a system are working as they should, and "diagnostic listening," which experts use to identify internal problems based on a taxonomy of aberrant sounds.[41] These two modes of listening are constantly happening all around us, and they are crucial to the maintenance and care of the city's technical and social infrastructures.[42] Civil engineers, for example, listen to ambient vibrations, harmonic excitations, and wave propagation to detect structural weaknesses in buildings and bridges and transit beds. And advanced instruments help us listen across urban scales that are not easily heard by human ears or bodies. Researchers in Alister Smith's Listening to Infrastructure lab at Loughborough University study sensors that monitor high-frequency "acoustic emissions" from "geotechnical assets" (buried pipelines, foundations, retaining structures, tunnels, and dams) in order to assess their condition, locate weakness, and target maintenance work.[43]

This applied research extends a tradition among artists who have sounded out infrastructural elements. For the centennial of the Brooklyn Bridge, in 1983, Bill Fontana mounted eight microphones under the bridge's steel grid roadway and broadcast live sounds at the World Trade Center plaza. In 1999, Stephen Vitiello spent six months in residence on the 91st floor of the World Trade Center, recording how Tower One swayed and creaked with the wind. Such works make sensible the micro-rhythms and macro-scale physical stresses that infrastructures withstand and amplify the distinct mechanics of their materials and construction techniques.[44] Other artists have encouraged listening to technical and media infrastructures, such as WiFi networks, cell connections, and the global positioning system. Since 2004, Christina Kubisch has hosted "Electrical Walks" in several dozen cities. Participants wear specially designed headphones that translate electromagnetic signals into audible sounds, disclosing the waves and particles—generated by activities like ATM transactions and CCTV surveillance—which perpetually envelop and penetrate urban bodies. Similarly, Shintaro Miyazaki and Martin Howse use logarithmic detectors, amplifiers, and wave-filter circuits to transform electromagnetism into sound, revealing the "rhythms, signals, fluctuations, oscillations and other effects of hidden agencies within the invisible networks of the 'technical unconscious.'"[45]

This work to auscultate infrastructure, to render it sensible, helps us appreciate how much listening we have ceded to machines. Turbines, windmills, freezers, vent fans, and hard-to-access machines in the off-limits "clean rooms" of pharmaceutical and tech manufacturing facilities—all signal their health to system operators by chugging along with a consistent tone and rhythm. AI can purportedly predict and prevent infrastructural snafus by scanning for idiosyncrasies within high-performance systems.[46] Some players in the predictive analytics field build training sets with sound samples of well-behaved machines, while others listen across a wide array of systems, identify anomalies, and then invite human engineers to help them analyze and classify the aberrant sounds. Humans also play a mediating role as liaisons between automated sonic analysis and the deployment of emergency services or maintenance workers. A manager overseeing a water treatment plant during a violent storm might rely on a dashboard of sonic alerts to pinpoint mechanical failures and then dispatch staff—or robots—to fix the problem. In the future, this auscultative agent might be the only human in the facility. . . .

Sarah Barns proposes that we recognize the future city as a "complex field of cognition, computation, desire and experience," an assemblage of vibrating, resonating, listening, sounding machines and bodies, including those of other species.[47] The polyphonic city contains many distinct ways of sensing and knowing, of diagnosing and healing, our selves and our spaces. Perhaps listening machines—rather than making scripted determinations about what "meaningful" information is extracted from the sonic environment—could be recruited by cities or community groups or artists to amplify the messy richness of that assemblage, or to highlight the machines' own subjectivity, or to compel us to listen to ourselves, and our machines, *listening*.[48]

Attending to whole ecologies, rather than specific sounds, reminds us that we live amid great biodiversity, and that listening can be a means of caring for those ecologies, rather than controlling or disciplining them.[49]

[Reproduced from "The Pulse of Global Passage: Listening to Logistics", in *Assembly Codes: The Logistics of Media*, ed. Matthew Hockenberry et al. (Duke University Press, 2021), © Shannon Mattern, 2021, reproduced by arrangement with Duke University Press; "Ear to the Wire: Listening to Historic Urban Infrastructures," in "Network Archaeology," *Amodern 2* (October 2013), https://amodern.net/article/ear-to-the-wire/, © Shannon Mattern, 2013, reproduced by arrangement with *Amodern*; "Urban Auscultation; or, Perceiving the Action of the Heart," *Places Journal* (April 2020), https://placesjournal.org/article/urban-auscultation-or-perceiving-the-action-of-the-heart/?cn-reloaded=1, © Shannon Mattern, 2020, reproduced by arrangement with *Places Journal*]

NOTES

1 Alberto Toscano, "Lineaments of the Logistical State," *Viewpoint Magazine*, September 28, 2014, https://viewpointmag.com/2014/09/28/lineaments-of-the-logistical-state/.

2 Recent work on "distant listening," which takes inspiration from the literary-critical methods of close and distant reading, has been applied across literary criticism, history, music, radio, and sound studies. [I once shared a partial bibliography on Twitter, but the tumultuous political economy of social media has impeded the logistics of digital cross-referencing.]

3 Henry Mayhew, *The Great World of London* (London, 1857), 35.

4 Thais C. Morata et al., "Noise Exposure and Hearing Disorders," in *Occupational and Environmental Health: Recognizing and Preventing Disease and Injury*, ed. Barry S. Levy et al. (Oxford University Press, 2011), 468.

5 For more on market noise, see Shannon Mattern (@shannonmattern), "On the continuing role of noise in an economy based on algorithmic transactions and high-frequency trades," Twitter, March 28, 2019, 11:46 p.m., https://twitter.com/shannonmattern/status/1111474659160195073.

6 Charmaine Chua, "The Quiet Port Is Logistics' Nightmare," *Empire Logistics*, September 21, 2015, https://www. empirelogistics.org /dispatches/ the-quiet-port.

7 John Durham Peters, *The Marvelous Clouds: Toward a Philosophy of Elemental Media* (University of Chicago Press, 2015), 62.

8 Charmaine Chua, "Landlessness and the Life of Seamen," *Empire Logistics*, September 28, 2015, empirelogistics.org /dispatches/landlessness-and-the-life-of-seamen. Nick Anderman, who's also traveled aboard a container ship, describes the sound of "maritime metal . . . twisting and flexing against oceanic forces." He wonders what these sounds "might tell us about the global flows of capital that underpin the movement of the ship in the first place?" Nick Anderman, "Sounding Maritime Metal: Listening to Global Trade at Sea," presented at the Society for Social Studies of Science, Boston, August 31, 2017.

9 Deborah Cowen, *The Deadly Life of Logistics: Mapping Violence in Global Trade* (University of Minnesota Press, 2014), 1.

10 Cowen, *Deadly Life of Logistics*, 111.

11 See, for instance, Anja Kanngieser, "Tracking and Tracing: Geographies of Logistical Governance and Labouring Bodies," *Environment and Planning D: Society and Space* 31 (2013).

12 Jesse LeCavalier, *The Rule of Logistics: Walmart and the Architecture of Fulfillment* (University of Minnesota Press, 2016), 164.

13 LeCavalier, *Rule of Logistics*, 167.

14 LeCavalier, *Rule of Logistics*, 166.

15 Cowen, *Deadly Life of Logistics*, 126.

16 Claudio Coletta and Rob Kitchin, "Algorhythmic Governance: Regulating the 'Heartbeat' of a City Using the Internet of Things," *Big Data and Society* (July-December 2017): 11. Algorhythmics is a reference to the media-archaeological "machine listening" work of Shintaro Miyazaki. [See Shintaro Miyazaki, "AlgoRHYTHMS Everywhere: A Heuristic Approach to Everyday Technologies," in *Off Beat: Pluralizing Rhythm*, ed. Jan Hein Hoogstad and Birgitte Stougaard Pedersen, Thamyris/Intersecting: Place, Sex and Race 26 (Brill, 2013). See also Shintaro Miyazaki, "Urban Sounds Unheard-of: A Media Archaeology of Ubiquitous Infospheres," *Continuum: Journal of Media & Cultural Studies* 27, no. 4 (2013). Miyazaki explains that "Algorhythms are vibrational, pulsed and rhythmized signals constituted both by transductions of physical fluctuations of energy and their oscillations as well as by abstract and logical structures of mathematic calculations. Algorhythms act in-between the . . . hardware and software" (ibid., 519).]

17 John Mannes, "The Sound of Impending Failure," *Tech Crunch*, January 29, 2017, techcrunch.com/2017/01/29/the-sound-of-impending-failure/.

18 Donna Haraway, "Situated Knowledges: The Science Question in Feminism and the Privilege of Partial Perspective," *Feminist Studies* 14, no. 3 (Autumn 1988): 581.

19 Haraway , "Situated Knowledges," 585.

20 Wesley Goatley, personal communication, June 5, 2018.

21 Nadia Drake, "Archaeoacoustics: Tantalizing, but Fantastical," *Science News*, February 17, 2012, https://www.sciencenews.org/view/generic/id/338543/ description/Archaeoacoustics_Tantalizing_but_fantastical; see also Chris Scarre and Graeme Lawson, eds., *Archaeoacoustics* (McDonald Institute for Archaeological Research, 2006). Sensory history has addressed similar epistemological and methodo-logical concerns; see Mark M. Smith, "Producing Sense, Consuming Sense, Making Sense: Perils and Prospects for Sensory History," *Journal of Social History* 40, no. 4 (2007).

22 Carlotta Daro, "Networked Cities: Infrastructures of Telecommunication and Modern Urban Theories" (presentation, Canadian Communication Association Conference, Media History Symposium, June 2010). See Hillel Schwartz, *Making Noise: From Babel to the Big Bang and Beyond* (Zone Books, 2011), on the visual and sonic impact of the proliferation of overhead wires (333, 428). Thoreau has also famously opined on the "celestial" sounds produced by these infrastructural aeolian harps.

23 Jean Gottman, "Megalopolis and Antipolis: The Telephone and the Structure of the City," in *The Social Impact of the Telephone*, ed. Ithiel de Sola Pool (MIT Press, 1977); Stephen Graham and Simon Marvin, eds., *Splintering Urbanism: Networked Infrastructures, Technological Mobilities and the Urban Condition* (Routledge, 2001), 50–51. Architectural historian Emily Bills also tells a fascinating story about the central role played by multiple, unconnected independent phone companies in agricultural production in late nineteenth-/early twentieth-century Los Angeles. She argues that "the telephone should be recognized as the first form of infrastructure to efficiently and effectively bind the greater Los Angeles area into a comprehensive, multinucleated whole" (Emily Bills, "Connecting Lines: L.A.'s Telephone History and the Binding of the Region," *Southern California Quarterly* [Spring 2009]).

24 Lewis Mumford, "What Is a City?" *Architectural Record* (November 1937).

25 Henri Lefebvre, *Rhythmanalysis: Space, Time and Everyday Life*, trans. Stuart Elden and Gerald Moore (Continuum, 2004).

26 Shannon Mattern, "Databodies in Codespace," *Places Journal*, April 2018.

27 Dan Ellis, "A History and Overview of Machine Listening," Computational Audition Workshop, London, May 12–14, 2010. Ellis made this proclamation a decade ago, but it still rings true, or "echoes."

28 "Makes Quiet Zones for City Hospitals," *New York Times*, June 24, 1907; and Emily Thompson, *The Soundscape of Modernity: Architectural Acoustics and the Culture of Listening in America, 1900 to 1930* (MIT Press, 2002), 121.

29 Karin Bijsterveld, *Mechanical Sound: Technology, Culture and Public Problems of Noise* (MIT Press, 2008), 101.

30 Karin Bijsterveld, "The Diabolical Symphony of the Mechanical Age: Technology and Symbolism of Sound in European and North American Noise Abatement Campaigns, 1900–40," *Social Studies of Science* 31, no. 1 (2001): 52; Bijsterveld, *Mechanical Sound*, 108–10; and Karin Bijsterveld, "'The City of Din': Decibels, Noise, and Neighbors in the Netherlands, 1910–1980," *Osiris* 18 (2003): 184. See also Leonardo Cardoso, *Sound-Politics in São Paolo* (Oxford University Press, 2019), 50–54.

31 Rogers H. Galt, "Results of Noise Surveys: Part I. Noise Out-of-Doors," *Journal of the Acoustical Society of America* 2, no. 1 (1930); Michael Mopas, "Howling Winds: Sound, Sense, and the Politics of Noise Regulation," *Canadian Journal of Law and Society* 34, no. 2 (2019).

32 Bijsterveld, *Mechanical Sound*, 110.

33 Cardoso, *Sound-Politics in São Paolo*, 54.

34 David Owen, "Is Noise Pollution the Next Big Public Health Crisis?," *The New Yorker*, May 6, 2019. See also the SONYC website, https://wp.nyu.edu/sonyc/.

35 Juan P. Bello et al., "SONYC: A System for Monitoring, Analyzing, and Mitigating Urban Noise Pollution," *Communications of the ACM* 62, no. 2 (February 2019): 2; Mark C. Cartwright et al., "Sonyc Urban Sound Tagging (SONYC-UST): A Multilabel Dataset from an Urban Acoustic Sensor Network," in *Proceedings of the Detection and Classification of Acoustic Scenes and Events 2019 Workshop (DCASE2019)*, ed. Michael Mandel et al. (New York University, 2019).

36 On performance-based planning and zoning, see Douglas C. Baker et al., "Performance-Based Planning: Perspectives from the United States, Australia, and New Zealand," *Journal of Planning Education and Research* 25 (2006); Daniel Doctoroff, "The Shared City: How Technology Will Improve

Urban Living," MAS Summit, New York, NY, October 22–23, 2015; Sidewalk Labs, "Zoning: The Legal and Social Codes of Urban Planning," September 21, 2017; and Luc Wilson et al., "Quantifying the Urban Experience: Establishing Criteria for Performance Based Zoning," SimAUD, Delft (2017). Today, many cities combine objective and subjective measures in developing acoustic planning models and enforcing noise abatement policies: certain types of noise, or noises that produce certain effects, might be prohibited, along with noises that exceed a particular quantitative measurement level. See Mopas, "Howling Winds," 314. A noise complaint can be substantiated by a resident's narrative testimony, e.g. that the neighbor's thumping bass causes headaches and nausea, even if it doesn't rate high on a decibel meter.

37 "Panacousticon" is drawn from Peter Szendy's *All Ears: The Aesthetics of Espionage*, trans. Roland Végsö (Fordham University Press, 2016). Thanks to Brian Miller and Julie Napolin for the reference.

38 Björn W. Schuller et al.,"COVID-19 and Computer Audition: An Overview on WhatSpeech & Sound Analysis Could Contribute in the SARS-CoV-2 Corona Crisis," preprint, March 24, 2020, https://doi.org/10.48550/arXiv.2003.11117.

39 Kadija Ferryman and Mikaela Pitcan, "Fairness in Precision Medicine," *Data & Society Report* (2018); Celia B. Fisher, "Will Research on 10,000 New Yorkers Fuel Future Racial Health Inequality?," *The Ethics and Society Blog*, August 30, 2016.

40 Tom Rice, "Listening," in *Keywords in Sound*, ed. David Novak and Matt Sakakeeny (Duke University Press, 2015).

41 Karin Bijsterveld, *Sonic Skills: Listening for Knowledge in Science, Medicine and Engineering (1920s–Present)* (Palgrave Macmillan, 2019), 77. See also Karin Bijsterveld, *Sound and Safe: A History of Listening Behind the Wheel* (Oxford University Press, 2014); Stefan Krebs, "'Sobbing, Whining, Rumbling': Listening to Automobiles as Social Practice," in *The Oxford Handbook of Sound Studies*, ed. Trevor Pinch and Karin Bijsterveld (Oxford University Press, 2012), 94; and Shannon Mattern, "Things That Beep: A Brief History of Product Sound Design," *Avant*, August 22, 2018.

42 See Shannon Mattern, "Maintenance and Care," *Places Journal* (November 2018).

43 Stephane Hans et al., "Dynamic Auscultation of Buildings and Seismic Integrity Threshold Assessment," First European Conference on Earthquake Engineering and Seismology, Geneva, Switzerland, September 3–8, 2006;

Jean-Paul Kurtz, *Dictionary of Civil Engineering* (Kluwer Academic Publishers, 2004), 46–47; F. Lamas-Lopez et al., "Geotechnical Auscultation of a French Conventional Railway Track-Bed for Maintenance Purposes," *Soils and Foundations* 56, no. 2 (April 2016); and Stuart Nathan, "Soil Squeaks Give Early Warning of Infrastructure Collapse," *The Engineer*, October 23, 2019.

44 Stephen Vitiello, in Kurt Anderson, "The Sounds of the World Trade Center," *The World,* August 14, 2013.

45 Christina Kubisch, "Invisible/ Inaudible: Electrical Walks: Electromagnetic Investigations in the City," https://christinakubisch.de/electrical-walks; and Miyazaki, "Urban Sounds Unheard-of."

46 Mannes, "The Sound of Impending Failure;" and Ben Popper, "Listening to Machines to Understand Why They Break," *The Verge,* January 11, 2017. See also the company Augury, which "combines the foundations of asset performance management (APM) and predictive maintenance (PdM) with the most recent advances in sensor technology"—including vibration, ultrasonic, temperature, and magnetic sensors—and artificial intelligence. "Machine learning algorithms compare your machine data to tens of thousands of recordings in our ever-growing database to detect anomalies and diagnose equipment malfunctions."

47 Sarah Barns, "Responsive Listening: Negotiating Cities of Sirens, Smartphones and Sensors," in *Sound, Media, Ecology,* ed. Milena Droumeva and Randolph Jordan (Palgrave Macmillan, 2019), 227. See also the work of Antonella Radicchi and Australia's National Acoustic Observatory Project, as presented in Lexy Hamilton-Smith, "Acoustic Observatory Will Record 'Galaxy of Sounds' to Help Scientists Monitor Australian Wildlife," *ABC News,* November 26, 2019. Thanks to Rowan Wilken for the observatory reference.

48 I'm grateful to all the folks on Twitter who responded to my request (December 2, 2019) for artists who work in critical AI.

49 Alison J. Fairbrass et al., "CityNet: Deep Learning Tools for Urban Ecoacoustic Assessment," *Methods in Ecology and Evolution* 10 (2019); Alice Eldridge et al., "Toward the Extraction of Ecologically-Meaningful Soundscape Objects: A New Direction for Soundscape Ecology and Rapid Acoustic Biodiversity Assessment," International Workshop on Big Data Sciences for Bioacoustic Environmental Survey (2015); and Alice Eldridge and Chris Kiefer, "Toward a Synthetic Acoustic Ecology: Sonically Situated, Evolutionary Agent Based Models of the Acoustic Niche Hypothesis," in *ALIFE 2018: The 2018 Conference on Artificial Life,* July 23–27 (MIT Press, 2018). Thanks to Ezra Teboul for the last reference.

The Ear and the Bridge: A Sonic Exploration of Placemaking Aboveground

Nadine Schütz

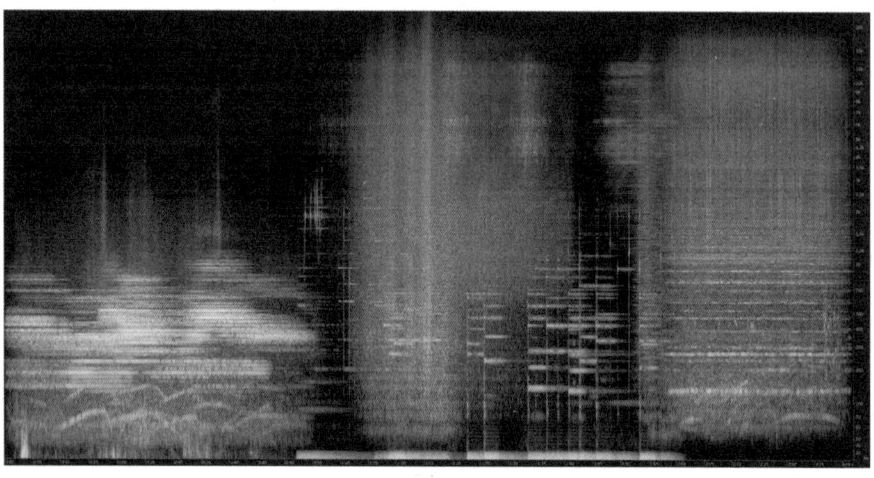

Spectrogram of the three elementary instruments recorded in context,
Nadine Schütz, 2024

Promenade Sonore: Vent, Soleil, Pluie *(2024)—a three-part sound work by Nadine Schütz integrated into the new Pleyel Bridge (Franchissement Urbain Pleyel) in Saint-Denis, France*[1]

SITUATEDNESS ABOVEGROUND

A bridge is, by its nature, a transient space, elevated aboveground, exposed to the sky, often traversed in haste. Yet bridges offer more than just physical connectivity; they create suspended experiences, allowing us to encounter the extremities of distance and proximity. They reveal unseen perspectives of their surroundings while simultaneously constraining our bodies' range of motion within their limited material boundaries. Situated within these contrasts, perhaps more intensely than elsewhere, we may sense the connection between the physical vibrations oscillating in the air that also continuously flow through these seemingly inert foundations of our urbanized environments. Achieving this state of situatedness means immersing ourselves in the present moment of being on the bridge, whether stationary or in motion.

These reflections do not arise from abstract considerations but from direct engagement with a specific context and an ears-on artistic challenge. Can sound convey or enhance a sense of place in a suspended structure? Can an auditory sensation give rise to a specific landscape experience aboveground? My sonic response to this challenge of placemaking, realized with the new Pleyel Bridge in Saint-Denis, is driven by an exploration of auditory, spatial, and environmental relationships. The tangible outcome is, of course, best experienced on-site. However, as I present the work here—now completed and open to the public—I interweave some of the methodological, conceptual, and theoretical considerations that shaped the eight-year process of its creation.

BASELINE

The land sound artwork Vent, Soleil, Pluie *is a sonic promenade in three parts, imagined and composed by sound artist Nadine Schütz for the public space that is the Pleyel footbridge. Three instruments were explicitly created for the three supporting structures, each corresponding to a meteorological element. Together, they make a harmonic landscape ambience that enhances and varies the perception of the site's materiality, spatiality, and climate. Wind, sun, and rain are the musicians.*[2]

In 2016, architect/engineer Marc Mimram invited me to collaborate on designing a new 300-meter-long bridge in Saint-Denis, intended to span the tracks dividing the Pleyel neighborhood from the rest of the town. Saint-Denis, a suburb directly connected to northern Paris, would later become a focal point for urban development tied to the 2024 Paris Olympics. At its initiation, however, the project was not shaped by this future event. It was driven by the pressing needs of mobility and urban repair in an area undergoing profound postindustrial transformation, yet still profoundly marked by the urban divides created by significant infrastructure. Its ambition was to create more than a functional link; it sought to establish an actual piece of city, fostering urban continuity.

How can sound help offer a specific, localized landscape experience that invites rest and pause within a piece of urban infrastructure that facilitates passage? This question framed my collaboration with Mimram, who envisioned the supporting structure as a central element shaping the bridge's identity as a place. Three spatialized beams rise above the generous pedestrian surface of the bridge and form elongated ovoid volumes conceived as inhabitable structures. The two larger structures are walkable metallic skeletons woven from arcs and fibers like the reversed hull of an uncovered ship. The third, smaller beam is clad in several centimeters of thick metal sheeting and fitted with a long concrete seating bench along its southern side.

SITE OF SOUND I

At the time of the design competition, the concept of a "site" was abstract: there was no tangible, accessible ground to stand on, only a zone suspended in the air, hovering above forty-two train tracks running north–south. This immaterial presence within a heavily material industrial context was even more striking given the limited accessibility of the adjacent grounds, where the site's intrinsic invisibility was heightened by its equally restricted audibility. To the west of the tracks, the SNCF Technicentre Landy operates around the clock, servicing trains departing from Paris-Nord, Europe's busiest railway station. This area is entirely off-limits to the public—like a pause in the urban landscape where trains remain stationary, undergoing maintenance.

By contrast, the eastern part of the train tracks is a zone of movement where trains pass, stop, and depart. This section integrates a station for regional trains with platforms connected by pedestrian overpasses. These overpasses, raised above the tracks, became my perch—my only means to "listen in" on what would become the immediate sonic environment, at least on this side of the future bridge. Melodic bows, squeaking single notes, howling crescendos, and endless decrescendos, interspersed with loudspeaker announcements carried away and distorted by the wind. Between these moments of sonic intensity lay stretches of humming silence, punctuated occasionally by sparse hammering from the train maintenance center.

This perched listening point also heightened my overall physical awareness, exposing my ears and body to the elemental forces of the environment: the movement of air, its temperature, shifting light, and the ever-changing meteorological conditions. It revealed to me the intrinsic physicality of what may be called the site; to convey a sense of place on the future bridge means embracing the specific environmental exposedness and amplifying the connection with this elemental, floating landscape—through sound. While the generous structural and architectural design of the pedestrian part of the Pleyel Bridge lays the foundations for it to function as a place that fosters diverse interactions, sound is to play a crucial role in situating it within the landscape—by creating resonance and response between the bridge's structural materiality, its immediate elemental surroundings, and the broader urban context.

WIND: AEOLIAN ORCHESTRATION

Inspired by an aeolian harp, the installation Vent *(Wind) turns the bridge into a string instrument, like an electric guitar, powered by the wind. Sixteen strings, mounted on the arches and tensioned by tuning keys, vibrate with the gusts, creating musical layers that intersect with the sounds of passing trains. Piezoelectric microphones transmit these resonances along the metal structure to the ground, where they emerge amplified, enriching the sound experience of the footbridge with a symphonic effect.*

The location I chose for the installation *Vent*, integrated in the largest inhabitable structure to the east of the bridge, corresponds, on the one hand, to the prospective study of air dynamics on the bridge conducted by the design team's environmental engineer, identifying the area most exposed to the winds. On the other, it aligns with the sonic and elemental landscape that most closely mirrors what I could hear and feel from my initial listening perch. Thus, the wind instrument is a direct acoustic and environmental response to this initial auditory and bodily site recognition. It meets with the harmonic complexity of railway dynamics through a spatialized arrangement of multiple sound-producing elements directed by wind forces. The sixteen aeolian strings of the *Vent* installation, spanning lengths of four, eight, and twelve meters, echo the rhythmic intervals of the structural arcs, each spaced four meters apart. Arranged in three groups along the north and south sides of the western edge of the curved structural volume, they form chords that shift subtly with variations in wind exposure. Different string diameters further enrich their aeolian reactivity, creating a dynamic interplay of tension and tone. This mechanical wind instrument is enhanced by an electroacoustic circuit, which I imagined like an aeolian memory, amplifying the strings' vibrations and layering them with triadic harmonized overtones. This airy symphony is then redistributed across twenty loudspeakers, seamlessly integrated into the wooden flooring. The spatial arrangement of the speakers mirrors and connects the physical placement of the string groups, weaving them into a unified sonic field, where layers of sound drift as though the bridge itself is breathing with the wind, converging together with the industrial tonalities of the railway flows to create a cohesive musical experience.

SUN: ENVIRONMENTAL RESONANCE

The installation Soleil *(Sun) uses the steel sheet of the supporting structure as the resonating body of an instrument. Like a loudspeaker membrane, the metal wall is brought to life by vibration transducers, creating sonic impressions that can also be felt by touch. The musical composition combines aquatic sounds digitally transposed into tonal textures and piano phrases, evolving with meteorological variations such as luminosity, temperature, and the changing seasons.*

The *Soleil* installation transforms the smallest, clad inhabitable structure, with its fifty-two-meter-long south-facing seating bench, into a resonant instrument. This instrument's keynote is shaped by the natural resonance effects, which are stimulated by twenty-two vibration transducers invisibly mounted on its surface behind the backrest of the bench. The environmental relationships embedded in the evolutive sonic composition emitted through this loudspeaker-like instrument extend to the wider urban context of the bridge and create a subliminal sonic geography.

The aquatic essence of the composition reflects the bridge's location between the Seine River and the Canal Saint-Denis. Initially based on field recordings from these waterways, the concept expanded to include natural and staged water sounds from across the world, echoing an intuitive reading of the train tracks as a river carrying stories from afar—a perspective shared with the architect. These natural acoustic sources are transposed into tonal textures using resonant filters that harmonize with the metal structure's natural resonances. Their transformation into piano phrases ties the composition to the Pleyel neighborhood, paying homage to its history as home to the Pleyel piano factory, which operated there from the mid-nineteenth century until 2013. The selective spectral analysis guiding this transposition is tuned to the harmonies of the nearby rain instrument, interweaving distant echoes of the bells.

Here, the sun's force does not directly create sound but is measured through luminosity and temperature sensors, while its trajectory is mapped using a calendar. This data is then transcribed to conduct an evolving environmental mix that shifts between natural and instrumental tonalities. The frequency composition of these sounds determines their perceived depth within the structural volume—the lower the tones, and the closer to the metal plate's resonant frequencies, the deeper their origin seems to be within. This resonance can be felt throughout your body when you lean your back against the opposite side of the structure, transforming sound into a tangible, physical experience.

RAIN: ELEMENTAL COUNTERPOINT

The installation Pluie *(Rain) transforms the footbridge into a vast percussion instrument animated by the rhythm of falling rain drops. Forty-nine suspended cymbals, each incorporating handpan-style cavities, capture the ephemeral impacts of rain and convert them into harmonic textures. Tuned to C-sharp minor, they play in perfect harmony with the bells of the Sacré-Coeur and the Saint-Denis Basilica.*

As with the wind instrument, in the installation *Pluie*, the elemental force—falling water droplets—serves as the direct sound generator. The weather condition this installation honors does not typically invite people to pause and linger, at least not today. Yet, I imagine a near future where rain falling from the sky will again be celebrated as a precious gift. Unlike the more constant presence of sun and wind, rain's elemental expression is, by its nature, rarer and more ephemeral.

These varying temporalities of audibility and inaudibility find their counterpart in the distinct sculptural expressivity of the three installations. While the instrumental components of the sun installation remain invisible, the fluctuating sonic presence of the wind instrument is visually anchored by carefully designed tuning keys. The much less frequently heard rain instrument, by contrast, occupies the rawest of the inhabitable structures and asserts itself with a strong visual presence. Like a tree canopy or a giant chandelier, its monumental percussion set spreads high above pedestrians' heads, evoking the sound it produces under the rain. At its core, this expansive structure creates a kind of salon—an open space inviting social interaction, perhaps even dance, beneath the rhythmic cadence of falling water, turned at dry times into an imagined echo.

SITE OF SOUND II

Together, the three installations—rain, wind, and sun—transform the bridge into a living instrument, allowing the environment to resonate with its supporting structure and materiality. By converting natural phenomena into musical actors, they weave sonic layers into these elevated environments, composing a unique, ephemeral, floating, yet structurally anchored sonic landscape. Responding to elemental forces while harmonizing with the industrial sounds of railway activity and integrating tones from the broader surroundings, they situate the bridge as a place within a richly layered suburban landscape, extending its perceived spatial reach.

As a *Promenade Sonore* (Sonic Promenade)—a sequentially spatialized polyphony allowing for space and silence in between—they accompany the pedestrian's journey, inviting them to engage not only with the structure of the bridge and the world around it but also with the ephemeral and untethered qualities of the sound itself.

NOTES

1 Project credits: Artist (concept, design/creation, composition, and artistic production direction): Nadine Schütz (((Echora))); Public art commission: Plaine Commune/Plaine Commune Développement; Architect/Engineer (bridge design): Marc Mimram; Environmental engineer: Franck Boutté; Production and installation of the artwork: Citynox, Music Unit, Écouter Voir, Idéal Pose; Construction manager: Artelia; General contractors: Bouygues Travaux Publics, Maeg

2 The framed sections correspond to the text (originally in French) on the title plaques affixed to the bridge's structure, which present the overall sound work as well as each individual installation.

Sounding Out

Cole Swensen

crossing great distances, though they be various, to settle as presence inciting attention: a sonic impression, and the body is suddenly on alert. The sternum as soundboard (sound is stored in the breastbone)—one is, after all, if nothing else, a musical instrument. At first felt rather than heard. Played by the wind. Played by everything, anything, by all that passes, birds. Pass glancing—they combine with wind into a kind of whistling—it's a blue kind—a blue of a hue you can hear in your bones. Though not in all of them; in fact, in only three, deep in the inner ear. These will reappear.

But back to the birds—this time they're on a wire, all in a line—picture the scene: birds, wires, and electricity streaming through everything—who will be the first to be heard? Given the cadence inherent to any living thing, given the fact that there is no thing alive that does not have its own internal beat, its own inherent rhythm—and you start tapping your foot, keeping time—which lets the bird that walked out onto the wire with something in mind create a mind.

But how does all this relate to you? We started out talking about the human body as a musical instrument—it's fundamental, contrapuntal. What is that creature in your chest (another bird?) keeping time to the entire outside world, and just how many of them are there? We'll put that question aside for the moment and notice the sound of a tear running down into your ear.

Which brings us back to those three tiny bones—the smallest in the human body, which encourages us to hone our inquiries—get more details, the specific name of each one, etc. We'll have to track them down. They will be made known. We'll hold them up to the light of the sun. We'll hold them up with tiny ivory tweezers, and they will shine. Aside: Though the sound they make, though a sting in the air, is also a scar—back to that tear—as in a rent that sang a fear. You know, I once dreamt that I once had a dream that singing was a tactile thing—and then there was that riot in the ear. It was your ear, and I reached out and tried to touch it, but all I could touch was a bit of tender flesh

Which passed in a gust, and I heard it through my hands.

2

The ear enters and spreads—enters a field and the birds fly off. The birds launch out over water, and the ear, too, launches out across it, turning the water to rain, which then turns it to something running, something in the distance, the infinitesimal footsteps, endless and striking a rhythm that lulls you to sleep. Distance will become an increasingly important character in this piece; in fact, distance will relentlessly follow us, but then it always does. And the ear tracks it—the ear and its early answer: *malleus, incus,* and *stapes*—the ossicles, my oracle, and the ear slouches off on its own, goes
back to the birds again.

(The birds, too, already so present, will only become more so.)

3

In many cultures, divination has been practiced by tossing the bones of the inner ear down onto a sheet of very flat, very white cloth and then reading the shadows they cast. The bones can be taken from any animal, though the smaller they are, the more detailed their information. Those of the bumblebee bat, with the smallest skull of any mammal, are highly prized and are said to whisper their information so softly that you have to lean down and actually touch them with your ear.

That ear, that eggshell ear, so often compared to a shell lying on a shore with the sun pouring through. There it is, your ear, basking on the beach, listening to the screeching of the gulls overhead, reeling through their acrobatic routines. It's time to bring them down to earth, arrange them in a circle, all facing outward and bid them be silent. Silent seagulls are so uncommon that they silence the sea as well. Now it's absolutely still, which allows the ear to plane along, just above the surface of the pacified ocean.

As the ear glides, hearing slides out in front of it, picking out details and detaching them, breaking them down into their smallest audial units and then reconstructing them into previously inaudible, and thus unthinkable, things, which they've now made accessible simply because now we can hear them: unraveling trees, night braided with light, hands turning ash into trees again, light melting into night into flight.

Which brings us back to the bumblebee bat and, more particularly, to its echolocation. We all use sound to find ourselves in the dark, and so we find each other, off on a wander, just as later, dogs barking in the distance down a road—that's what they're doing—taking soundings—as do train whistles miles away, causing an instant deepening of evening, even in the middle of the day—one that's more internal than out there in the vast spaces, which they continually increase.

There are sounds, not many, but a few, that inherently create distance; they don't only extend it; they actually manufacture more of it. We've touched on a couple—the barking of dogs, the whistle of a train—in both cases, the distance increases according to the degree that you can't see the dog or the train. All the power of seeing is then transferred and added to that of hearing. There are also birds (we said they'd return), for instance, owls, that have the capacity to create distance through sound—and just to stress, this is not metaphoric or impressionistic—it's real mileage that they create by casting their calls outward at just the right pitch that they set off at a velocity that irrepressibly creates an elastic increase in appreciable space.

And there are other birds as well—crows, in fact, constitute the epitome of this principle; their caws extend endlessly, and when gathered in a murder, again, arrange them in a circle, nine of them all facing outward, and clap three times. There's a cacophony that strikes a pure harmony, and there you have it, a perfect sphere of swirling crows, unraveling everything. In all of these cases, the sound—caw, whistle, bark—must already be at some distance, as they multiply on an exponential relay principle, and in all cases, darkness greatly augments the process, and while at night, it's much more active than in the day, it's oddly at dusk, just when light and dark are perfectly in balance, that the effect is the strongest. You can travel immeasurable distances when just that point is struck.

Exactly how dusk operates on the ear and, even more, on the phenomenon of extension that only the ear can perceive, or provide, has not yet been determined, though numerous studies are currently underway. Studies are also researching what happens if the crows, the dogs, and the train all go off at once. Oddly enough, they seem to cancel each other out, and there you are, in perfect suspension, going nowhere. But if it's only two—say, crows and train whistle or barking dogs and crows—you begin once more to plane in a clean, light line just inches above the extending distance.

And the distance doesn't only extend—it also augments in dimension, so that a sounding's usually linear spear becomes spherical and eventually goes beyond the physical, and distance enters other modalities, the emotional, the historical, the temporal. And it was just as I was entering the temporal one evening that I watched a crow leaving my field of sight at exactly the moment that a dog I couldn't see barked in the deepening distance, and there it went, all of it, off with the bird, who carried it away and will use it, and will use it well.

Stories of a River in Transformation

Laure Brayer (AAU-CRESSON),
translated by Benjamin Connor

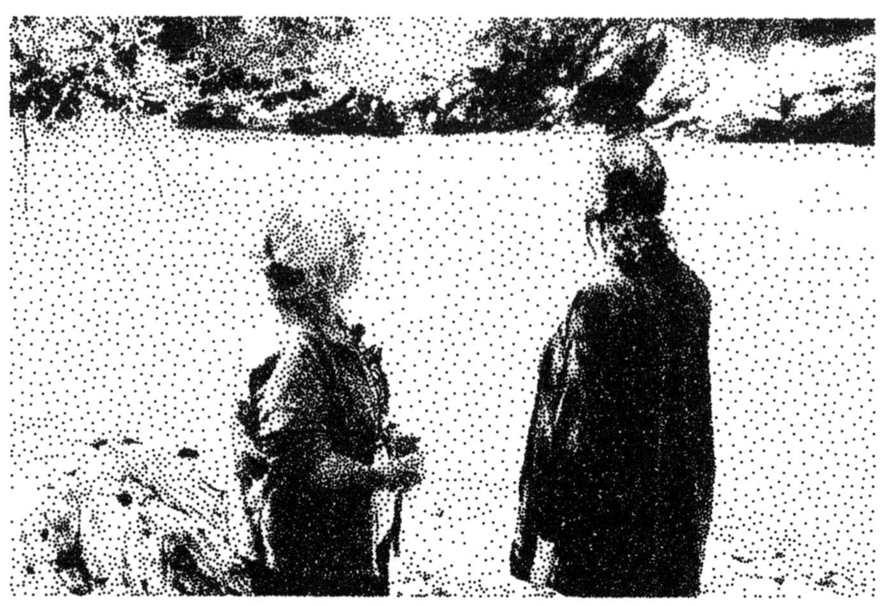

Interview with local resident, Laure Brayer

ARRIVAL IN A CHANGING VALLEY

In the lower Romanche valley, a highway winds its way through an Alpine dale. The road runs alongside a tumultuous river, where small islands of rocky debris can be glimpsed being swept away by the current. At several points, the road crosses the raging river without this slowing the speed of the traffic; bypasses skirt the villages, flood zones, and landslide risk areas. The mountain is collapsing here, with rocks continually tumbling down the steep slopes.

Upstream, the massifs on either side of the valley narrow even more, transforming it into a slender passage with gorges carved out by the Romanche. The road veers away from the water, traversing the small towns of Livet-et-Gavet that are strung out along its path. Hydroelectric infrastructure from the past century can be seen through the window: rusted penstocks line the riverbanks, massive surge tanks dot the landscape, a roadside canal suddenly goes airborne, the white foam of a spillway tints the area around a dam, electric cables streak the sky from pylon to pylon, and bright-yellow signs warn that the water may rise suddenly owing to power plant activity. Also visible are the remains of abandoned factories, workers' housing estates that are still inhabited, and communal buildings built by Charles Albert Keller, the prosperous engineer and industrialist who set in motion the valley's hydroelectric development in the early twentieth century.

Countless construction trucks noisily punctuate the traffic: colored dump trucks with open beds full of stony rubble crisscross the valley, heading to the open area where the rock debris disgorged by tunnel-boring machines is temporarily stored. This is Électricité de France (EDF)'s largest construction site in the country: the Romanche-Gavet project, which is carving out portions of the mountain to lay a ten-kilometer-long headrace tunnel that will divert water from the Romanche to a new underground power plant, one that will generate more power than all of the old facilities combined. This new facility will soon replace them, and as old dams and hydroelectric plants are demolished, they will make way for a renaturation project that will bring native plant species back to the riverbanks and create a cycle path linking Grenoble and the Oisans massif.

*

The river has a torrential flow—we hear noise, crashing, rolling boulders. It's a kind of violence being expressed, accentuated by the resonance chamber effect of the mountain.[1]

We hear and see rocks tumbling down the cliff!

One night we heard a loud noise. One whole face of the mountain had come down. There was dust and dirt all the way to the other side of the garage. Who wants to live here, with this never-ending noise?

In each factory there's a transformer, quietly humming.

Under the pylons there's a very specific sonic effect, like a crackling when it's humid out. I've never heard the siren for the Romanche.

Four years of excavating to dig the new headrace tunnel. The construction site was active twenty-four hours a day, and there was constant commotion. During construction, we could hear explosions.

Folks at the EDF construction site could predict when the water level would rise by listening to the "song of the pebbles" rolled along by the Romanche.

*

THE WAVES OF THE WATER

It is in this context of landscape transformation that a collective of researchers (AAU-CRESSON) and artists (Regards des Lieux) came together, both interested in sensory perceptions, performances, and projects relating to the river.[2] Looking beyond the valley's tangible heritage and the conservation issues it faces, this art/research project aimed to interrogate the memories of those who lived in and around the Romanche. How can those who live in the valley be witnesses, stakeholders, and transmitters of the memory of these places? What past, present, and potential sensory experiences does the river offer, complicating its image as a simple resource to be exploited?

The research and creative practices of different members of the project were all developed during a period of immersion: long-term residencies, creative workshops, and cultural events for Regards des Lieux, and in situ studies for the CRESSON researchers; these involved walking surveys, interviews, conversations with people while walking, as well as stories collected during the project's public events. A second shared point of interest was sound: Regards des Lieux bases its practice on the form of the cine-concert, where sonic composition is inspired by—and sometimes reenacts—in situ field recordings; CRESSON initially developed its research on lived space through the prism of sound, combining approaches from architecture, social science, and engineering to track the sensory, constructed, and social dimensions that make up the ambience of inhabited spaces.

At this time of massive change, what could we hear in the Romanche Valley?[3] What did these sonorities give us access to? And what forms did this journey mediated by sound take in the different phases of the research process? These are the questions we will address, discussing the scope of a sound-based approach for each phase of the research.

WALKING SURVEYS: LISTENING CLOSELY TO THE TERRITORY

We get out of the car at Livet-et-Gavet and walk toward the Romanche, which we can't see yet, the village having developed facing away from the water. At the far end of a large vacant lot, the emerging riparian forest invites us in. After a few steps, we are enveloped by the roaring of the river, which drowns out the sound of the highway and, rapidly, that of our voices. juL McOisans, our expert on *Sonic Experience: A Guide to Everyday Sounds*, tells us that this is a perfect example of what is known as the balcony effect.[4]

This effect—which is otherwise known as "limite ultime" (ultimate limit)[5]—"occurs when one moves from one sonic environment to another over a short distance, even simply by leaning forward and backward, on a balcony or parapet."[6] Here the steep riverbank acts as the parapet, instantly tipping the listener who approaches into the sonic world of the river. We walk in a state of floating attention, open to our multisensory perceptions. The sound of the Romanche carries so much information; it communicates its flow, the season, the mountainous area, the humidity of the air. Some of us have microphones, which will be used to create a qualitative description of the sonic ambiances of the different places we've traversed. Headphones on, Martin is recording and listening in a focused and amplified way that guides his path, leading him toward objects with sonic interest, like the humming electrical transformers we come across—which he will later work with in his compositions. Meanwhile, juL has put binaural microphones (or an "artificial head") in his ears, allowing a recording to be made that is as close to the human auditory experience as is possible. This method of recording has no direct impact on his movements: it is designed to be played back later, to serve as the basis of an audio analysis and as a moment of shared listening experience. In listening again to a fragment of sound recorded during this walk[7]—a group of children playing in the street, with the muffled noise of the highway and the Romanche in the background—an impression emerges: we hear the workers' housing estate, its narrow streets, uncrowded and without sidewalks, and the lives of its young residents unfolding there.

CONVERSATIONS WHILST WALKING: RECORDING STORIES IN RELATIONSHIP TO THE SOUND ENVIRONMENT

In a second phase of the project, residents and professionals living in the valley guided us along walking routes chosen by them to express their attachment to the river.[8] These walking interviews were recorded so that the words could be transcribed and the connection between the stories and the sonic space in which they emerged could be analyzed when the recordings were played back. The result is to bring out the predominant sonic presence of the river, which affects the body—we raise our voices in response to the volume and then go quiet and listen—and precedes visual experience, helping to give the river a significant sensory depth. This sonic signature, the result of a particular spatial configuration (of the gorges) and a specific moment in time, whether seasonal (the thawing of the snow upstream) or anthropogenic (water released from a dam), can provoke a variety of emotions, like fear, annoyance, or appreciation. The auditory experience of the Romanche is also tied to an ever-present vigilance for the warning sound that signals rising waters. The danger of the area near the river amplifies one's attention, giving rise to a unique sensory awareness, a sense of attachment, and even to river-related aesthetic considerations.

*

We don't see the rushing water, but we hear it. It's inextricably linked to the torrential flow, to the slope. Downstream, the sound is not nearly so loud.

With the torrential flow, when it moves, it really moves! There's noise, crashing, rolling boulders . . . it's really something. It's a kind of violence being expressed, and that can scare you.

For the first few years, the sound of the Romanche was an assault on my ears. I would say to myself: It won't shut up! When will they turn the water off?! Now, I don't hear it anymore.

It's bucolic here, with the trees. The sound of the road is covered by the sound of the Romanche. It does you good to listen to the river water. I really love the sound of the Romanche. It's part of our environment, it's pleasant.

*

PUBLIC EVENTS: INTERROGATING THE AUDITORY DIMENSION OF MULTISENSORY MEMORIES

Several workshops were held in public spaces to collectively create a map of sensory memories of the valley with local residents.[9] What do these sound memories (some of which are included in the introduction) reveal to us? Some are linked to human activity: hydroelectric sound-producing objects (transformers, pylons, alert systems), the EDF construction site (machines and vehicles), or highway traffic. Some have to do with the living mountain (rockfalls, animal activity), while others describe the signature sound of the Romanche (speed, topography, flow, area) and the song of its water, which produces specific emotional relationships. Accounts of sound memories often connect the identification of a source with a judgment or an expression of taste (discomfort, complaint, aesthetic approval), running the lexical gamut from "noise" to "music."

EXHIBITION AND PERFORMANCE: INTERPRETING THE SOUNDS OF THE ROMANCHE

The last phase of the research, in which sound takes on a new role, is sharing it with the public at large in the form of artistic and research creations. Through films and cine-concerts, as well as in selections of sound fragments (which are geotagged, dated, and annotated) shared through Cartophonies, a series of auditory portraits of the valley takes shape, expressing, in another form, complex experience of this place. As this area undergoes profound change, these auditory portraits create a contemporary sonic archive, documenting sounds that have recently disappeared: "Le chant des transfos" is a composition based on recordings of electrical transformers that are no longer operating.[10]

Dive into the sensory depths (both spatial and temporal) of the Romanche and reflect on its inherent complexity: that is what these riverside investigations and stories invite you to do. This sound-based approach allows for the intermingling of multiple dimensions of the sensory experience of the Romanche:

geographical and landscape context, the social practices of humans and other animals, development brought about by political and economic choices, historical and seasonal events, the listening conditions and sense memories of an attentive listener—these are all different facets of our relationship with the river, inviting us to think about its future.

NOTES

1 These words come from local residents and were collected in the making of the Sense Memory Map of the Romanche. While the stories evoked various sensory modalities, the fragments collected here refer to sound memories.

2 Laure Brayer et al., *Les Ondes de l'eau: Mémoires des lieux dans la vallée de la Romanche* (Naima, 2023)—an art/research project by Regards des Lieux and AAU-CRESSON, led by Laure Nicoladzé (cultural director) and Laure Brayer (scientific director), with Martin Debisschop, Ryma Hadbi, Jérémie Lamouroux, Sylvie Laroche, juL Mc Oisans, and Rachel Thomas: part of the program "Mémoires des XXe et XXIe siècles en Auvergne-Rhône-Alpes" (Memories of the Twentieth and Twenty-First Centuries in Auvergne-Rhône-Alpes), 2018 session of the Auvergne-Rhône-Alpes region and the Regional Directorate of Cultural Affairs.

3 From January 2019 to June 2021—i.e., before the dismantling of the hydraulic infrastructure began.

4 Jean-François Augoyard and Henry Torgue, eds., *Sonic Experience: A Guide to Everyday Sounds*, trans. Andra McCartney and David Paquette (McGill-Queen's University Press, 2005). Originally published as *À l'écoute de l'environnement: Répertoire des effets sonores* (Parenthèses, 1995). This directory, which CRESSON developed in the 1990s, facilitates the description, not of objects or auditory landscapes, but of sound phenomena relative to a context, local organization, and the conditions of perception.

5 Grégoire Chelkoff et al., *Prototypes sonores architecturaux: Méthodologie pour un catalogue raisonné et des expérimentations constructives* (CRESSON, 2003), 64.

6 Laure Brayer et al., *Ausculter l'environnement* (CRESSON, 2024), 145.

7 "Rioupéroux, course d'enfants," Cartophonies, accessed February 7, 2025, https://www.cartophonies.fr/sounds/2304/riouperoux-course-denfants/.

8 "ODE - Itinéraires en Romanche," Nakala, May 16, 2022, accessed February 7, 2025, https://nakala.fr/collection/10.34847/nkl.b8f37c1v.

9 "Carte des mémoires sensibles de la Romanche - version finale," accessed February 7, 2025, https://nakala.fr/10.34847/nkl.2bad8uj6.

10 "Le chant des transfos," Cartophonies, accessed February 7, 2025, https://www.cartophonies.fr/sounds/2319/le-chant-des-transfos/.

Listening to rue Lambert

Soline Nivet & Ariane Wilson,
translated by Benjamin Connor

[Sunday, October 13, 2024]

Dear Ariane,

I hope you're well. I imagine you'll see this message when you get back from your Baroque cello course in Tours. Surprisingly enough, even though we live so near to one another and teach classes one above the other on Tuesdays in the lovely building on rue Jacques Callot, we never manage to cross paths or catch up other than over email!

Paradoxically, we saw each other the most during the 2020 lockdown, when we instituted our daily walk through the twists and turns of Montmartre.

Do you remember that we managed to cover nearly seven kilometers within the authorized one-kilometer radius? I have such fond memories of our route—we walked it so many times and, in the end, thought we knew it inside out.

That's actually why I'm writing to you today. I have just discovered that if we had strayed slightly from our path by way of rue Lambert, we would have passed by no. 8.

I wonder what we would have said of it at the time.

Could you make a detour to pass by there sometime this week? It's right next to your apartment. Bring a tuning fork (Why not?).

All my best! Enjoy the rest of your Sunday.

Love,
Soline

[Thursday, October 17, 2024]

Dear Soline,

Because I persist in using neither signals nor waves to navigate the city, and because I didn't have *L'indispensable: Paris pratique par arrondissement* in my pocket, I went by the rule of my dear late friend, the walking artist Hendrik Sturm: ask for directions from the elderly and people who are walking their dogs. A lady who meets both criteria, seated on the lowest bar of some scaffolding in front of the laundromat, waiting for her laundry with her dachshund on a leash, tells me that rue Lambert is "not far, not far, toward the town hall." A man who only satisfies the first criterion assures me that "it's quite close. But where?"

In the end, I find it, set back from rue Ramey and rue Custine. It would indeed have been just slightly out of the way of our salutary daily walk, but it would have led us into the confines of a closed rectangle of streets.

It is the time of day when singing children clatter down the sidewalk, while their parents chatter away on their cell phones. A suspended hissing noise whizzes past me, and I think to myself that such a sound will be a keynote of the sonic landscape when all cars have gone electric. A medley of words crisscrosses the space in front of Café Iso on the corner, and a wave of rhythmic pulsing spills out of the MG17 restaurant. The noise fades, and there is something of a sonic hole, the kind that makes you feel as though you could fall into it, the acoustic equivalent of a chasm. It is no. 8, rue Lambert. I listen closely and hear nothing special. I'm surprised, considering you recommended that I bring a tuning fork.

The ground floor is separated into two shop windows by the door of the building, but these storefronts are clad entirely in louvered metal shutters. Obediently, they follow the rhythm of the neighbor-ing façades: blue slats on the bottom, then a middle section divided into four panels of white slats, then another blue section on top. I press my right ear to the panels and still hear nothing. The silence and dullness of the openwork façade make the sounds to my left all the more audible. "What a pain in the ass you are! You say you're coming and then you don't!" roars out from the phone of a passerby in a mid-length coat. Tires hiccup along the cobblestones arrayed in fan patterns. A drunkard thrusts his hand into the gutter, howling. It starts to rain. Raindrops patter on the taut membrane of my umbrella, so that I can no longer listen carefully from beneath its acoustic dome. I feel then that I seem suspicious. I walk up the street and come out on rue Nicolet. A printed text is pasted up on a wall:

In order for me to listen to poetry that isn't political, I must listen to the birds
And in order to hear the birds, the warplanes must be silent.
Marwan Makhoul, Palestinian poet

Love,
Ariane

- The original text of the Marwam Makhoul poem reads, "In order for me to *write* poetry that isn't political . . ." (italics added). The version printed above is taken directly from what is stenciled on the wall on rue Nicolet.

[Monday, October 28, 2024]

Dear Soline,

I'm writing to you again about no. 8, because I stopped by twice more during the week; rue Lambert is quite close to a little studio where I often go to practice the cello. The neighbors must be wondering about the regular visitor who puts her ear up to the shutter slats as one would to the screen of a prison visiting room. Still nothing, and so I am resolved to hear better.

Last Saturday, the 26th, I enlisted my friend Elsa. Not so long ago, I took part in a sound walk for which Elsa's Poumtchak Studio devised ear extensions so that we could listen through holes, grates, or windows. She arrives at no. 8 armed with one of these long tubes, sturdy yet flexible with colored endpieces to choose from: either a large amplification cylinder or a small directing nozzle.

It is 6:15 p.m. We begin with the naked ear. Storefront to the left of the entryway: silent. Storefront to the right of the entryway: surprise—a loud, low-frequency buzz pulsates from the central panels in the white section of the façade, more or less at ear level! Simultaneously, there is a current of warm air. The higher one raises one's hand, the warmer it feels. The lower one's hand goes, the colder. The panels on the far sides, the first and fourth, are neither warm nor buzzing. To investigate further, we use the listening tube, onto which we clip the small nozzle, which can easily be inserted between the slats. But the buzzing has stopped. Even with our apparatus, we hear nothing—not up high or down low or to the sides. Nothing but a light, sinusoidal breath of air—I think an F—caused by the listening tube.

6:35. Now the left storefront is the one buzzing! Elsa, with the listening tube, reports that the low-frequency noises are coming from the upper section of blue slats; from the top white section comes a trio of sounds that reminds her of a didgeridoo (the same low noises combined with a high-pitched whistle and the whoosh of the tube); from the lower blue section, nothing. The left storefront gives off less heat than the right-hand one.

6:40. Nothing more. On the right-hand storefront, the heat seems to have traveled upwards, but there is no more sound. The only thing that seems fairly certain to us is that the sound and heat are concentrated behind the central panels and start midway up the ground floor.

A woman who lives on rue Lambert stops, curious about what we're doing. "We're listening for what might be hidden behind the slats of this storefront," I tell her. "There used to be a print shop there," she tells us. "It was very noisy, much noisier than the server that replaced it a few years ago."

6:55. Now that we know the function of what is hidden behind the slats, we try again. Elsa hears a heartbeat, but I inform her that it's coming from the pulse of the music at the MG17 African restaurant.

7:00. Still nothing. The slats seem to have cooled off. To understand and chart the cycle and movements of the buzzing and of the heat between these two storefronts, we'd need to set up a twenty-four-hour watch. Are you ready to camp out?

7:25. We slip in behind two residents of the building, a young couple, and enter the tiny entrance hall. We ask them if they can hear ventilation noises from the courtyard when they're up in their apartment. They tell us there is no courtyard, just an extension of the ground floor. Did they know that they live above a server room? "Oh, no," they reply indifferently as they head upstairs. To the right of the staircase is a door with a sign reading "PLEASE DO NOT BLOCK ACCESS TO THIS ROOM." When we press our ears to the brown metal door, we detect white noise that lightly oscillates between what might be an E and a D. Around two meters back toward the entryway, that sound is drowned out by the higher-pitched noise of an electricity meter in a small white box. One of the mailboxes is still labeled with the name Hirech Printing. So the server won't reveal its name? We meditate on the fact that replacing the drumbeat of the print shop with a buzzing noise reflects a change in the medium of information.

See you tomorrow on rue Jacques Callot!

Ariane

P.S. Attached are a few photos from our expedition.

– Poumtchak Studio is a scenography and design-fiction/architecture research studio founded by the architects Charly Dufour and Elsa Lebrun.

[Sunday, November 3]

Dear Ariane,

How have you been since lunch on Tuesday with our colleagues from the School of Architecture? We can't seem to find any other time to see each other in the neighborhood and outside of work.

Thank you for your reply, and for the photos! I'm relieved to know I wasn't dreaming—there really is something going on at 8 rue Lambert. I took the opportunity over this long All Saints' Day weekend to go there myself and look around a bit, hoping I might find you there.

You weren't there, and the Beast was silent when I went by.

So, a woman told you it was a server? For now, I prefer to call it the Beast because of its sporadic breathing (perhaps it's holding its breath?), its warmth, and also because of the whales. Did you see fourteen blue whales stenciled onto a blue wall with the title

OCEANOCEANOCEANOCEAN
OCEANOCEANOCEANOCEANOCEANO
CEANOCEANOCEANOCEA

right next to the Marwan Makhoul poem? They reminded me of David Rothenberg's *Whale Music*, which I discovered only this morning (you must have known of it for years!) and which I've been listening to on repeat all day as I think about our conversation.

In the *Le Monde* weekend supplement, I came across an article about the work of Jérôme Sueur, a researcher at the Museum of Natural History, who uses the idea of "biophony" (a term borrowed from the American Bernie Krause, I believe) to organize and supervise eco-acoustic surveying and monitoring over very long periods of time in forests around the world. He studies ecosystems by recording them and inventorying their sounds; sadly, he also documents the gradual onset of silence and highlights the role that noise pollution plays in the physiology, behavior, and reproduction of some creatures who end up . . . mute.

Right after I read that, I listened to a podcast where Sueur touches on the relationship between ecoacoustics and music. Among the pieces that were played was a fabulous Rothenberg clarinet and whale piece that presents me with a small quandary that I'd like to tell you about soon.

But back to the Beast at 8 rue Lambert. I'd very much like to think about its ecosystem. To that end, could I ask two small favors of you? Look at the list of Wi-Fi networks that you could connect to from your home and send me a screenshot (I'm attaching what I just did at my apartment as a model).

And perhaps also follow the cable that goes from your router out to your landing, and see where it leads you: to the ground floor or to the basement of your building? Likewise, listen and take a photo?

Enjoy your Sunday evening.

Love,
Soline

– David Rothenberg, "Valentine's Day 1992," on *Whale Music*, Terra Nova, 2008.

– Podcast: "Jérôme Sueur, éco-acousticien: 'Les insectes ne font pas du bruit, c'est un paysage sonore instructif!'" June 26, 2022, France Musique, https://www.radiofrance.fr/francemusique/podcasts/musique-emoi/jerome-sueur-entomologiste-8999534.

– *Le Monde* article: Pierre Mouterde, "'Écouter' la forêt: Du Gâtinais au Jura, des micros pour mieux comprendre la biodiversité," *Le Monde*, November 3, 2024, https://www.lemonde.fr/planete/article/2024/11/03/ecouter-la-foret-du-gatinais-au-jura-des-micros-pour-mieux-comprendre-la-biodiversite_6373294_3244.html.

[Monday, November 25, 2024]

My dear Soline,

When I followed your instructions and took a picture of all the Wi-Fi networks that I can connect to from my apartment, several "B-Boxes" appeared at the top of the long list. For a moment I thought that might stand for *Baleine-Box* (Whale Box), before the subterranean expedition you encouraged me to take led me to deduce that B stood for Bouygues Telecom (the mix-up wasn't completely random, since in 2019 Bouygues invested in a company called Flying Whales).

But my router's network is Free. Let's start from the beginning. On the sixth floor, I took a still-life photograph: a tangled configuration of electric cables, a Philips cordless landline on a base, a Flip Lexon alarm clock, a lampstand, a Freebox Delta, an Altlab optical network terminal box, and two books: Jean-Claude Carrière's version of the *Mahabharata* and Auður Ava Ólafsdóttir's *Miss Iceland*. Still life is the right term, because the alarm clock is on "off," the cordless landline and the two boxes no longer work, and even the books—now finished—have been abandoned under these electronic ligaments.

On the landing of this attic floor, cables emerge from holes crudely drilled above three doors, which have cracked the plaster. From there, they run along the ceiling in complex interlacings, one hanging in an elegant parabola underneath the floor number placard, and finally they all run into a vertical PVC cable channel not far from the red fire extinguisher.

From floor to floor, the wires emerge from the top corner of the doors like slender tentacles and run into the cable channel. The number and type of boxes that connect to the channel varies by floor. As a novice observer, I'd classify them in four types: the small, square, silver box with a lock, the 3M distribution box, the Aiphone distribution box, and the Large Unmarked Box, which I will call a LUB.

Unlike the minimalist 3M boxes and LUBs, the Aiphone has much to say: "Made in Thailand"; "Model GT4Z"; "Lot TB87144R"; "Strip length 9 mm"; "Solid conductor"; "B1B2R1R2"; five "Line Out"s and a "Line In." I'm giving you every detail of these acronyms and numerals because they are elements of a secret script, the cryptic grammar familiar to a society of technicians, material objects, knowledge, and signs—and I feel completely lost in a foreign language whose codes escape me. (According to what I gleaned from a technophile neighbor, the small, square silver box is the telephone distribution frame, the LUB is a distribution frame for TV cables coming from the basement, the Aiphone box is a distribution frame for radio antennae on the roof, and the 3M box is an optical fiber distribution frame. There is also one large, old cast-iron box, apparently a distribution board.

On the ground floor is a former caretaker's lodge that has been converted into a studio just within the legal limits of square footage allowed for rental. The air thrums, sonic interference caused by the refrigeration unit a greengrocer is hiding in the courtyard, robbing the studio of any semblance of quiet. That tiny apartment feeds one more cable into the cable channel, which vanishes down into the tiled floor. I trace its route to the cellar, as you suggested. At the foot of the staircase are six Prysmian-brand boxes piled on top of each other. They each have small labels, which I'll list for you, starting from the top box: "free," "storage block," "client block nr 4," "operator fr no 4 (PMI 2313)," "SFR module," "Bouygues module."

A small yellow warning triangle is pasted on each box, with the word "laser" along the side of a drawing of what looks to me like a magician's black wand. In some of the boxes there are thin multicolored wires braided together, in others, coiled orange and green cables. Entering the cable channel from above are a series of gray, green, and black corrugated cable sleeves, labeled with plastic rings as one would a bird's leg or a farm animal's ear. One, marked SFR, gives a telephone number for emergencies and an address for the

Office of High-Speed Broadband: Quai du Pont-du-Jour in Boulogne-Billancourt. I wonder whether in your next email you'll send me to look around at this Ministry of New Digital Powers.

I keep following the cables in the basement as they trace the fine stone vaults of the first large cellar, running parallel to gas pipes and electrical wires. In the same room, I find a plastic box marked POB-PLA 75-085 12002. The internet tells me it's a Free Infra fiber-optic patch panel. The cables coming out of this box make an elegant loop around it, then rise toward the vaulted ceilings and join the run of cables from the aforementioned six boxes. This confluence of wires flows into a dead-end tunnel that's narrow and low, but nevertheless I can squeeze through it. The wires make a ninety-degree turn and disappear up into the stonework—my underground sense of direction tells me they're headed toward the street. Suddenly, my subconscious sense of gravitational flow inverts itself, and I realize that it all begins *here*, going from under the street up to the sixth floor, and not the other way around. Or rather, I actually no longer know which direction "the signs in wire networks" (Bruno Latour) travel in, drowning as I am in countless currents, wires, plastic boxes, plastic wall ties, cables, and plastic channels.

I listen, as you asked me to. In the vaulted cellar, the furtive whoosh of the tunnel; occasionally, several minutes of buzzing along with a subtle ultrasound from behind the wooden stake fence of cellar 6, which belongs to our grocer; the drumbeat of steps on the sidewalk above; the melody—muffled down here—that hails the beginning and end of classes at the nearby school; the lapping of water running through a pipe. I hear nothing from the boxes. Unless it's infrasound or ultrasound, I'm beginning to worry that my hearing is failing.

From the depths of the cellar, I think back to your whales and naturalist musicians. What a coincidence that our correspondence has led us here when on your birthday—Do you remember?—I once gave you George Crumb's *Vox Balaenae* among my selection of works that were written the year you were born. The American composer was inspired by the songs of humpback whales and wanted to evoke the "powerful, impersonal forces of nature." And for *my* last birthday, a friend gave me *A Book of Noises: Notes on the Auraculous* by Caspar Henderson, in which the author dedicates a chapter to whales. On page 112, he says that the cellist Lise Cristiani played Bach for whales in the Sea of Okhotsk in the middle of the nineteenth century. This delights me, since the intrepid cellist who brought her Stradivarius to Siberia is one of my heroines. I flip through her *Voyage to Siberia* and find the story of a July night in 1849:

> It was nighttime; we ran onto the deck breathlessly.
> "What? What is it?"
> "Look!"
> And we saw the monster quietly settled beneath the keel. Everyone, overtaken by the same sense of caution, began to speak in a whisper for fear of startling the impressionable animal that was carrying us. Finally, after catching its breath, the whale sank into the abyss, leaving a great whirlpool in its wake.
> We did not see it again until daylight, the sun on its back, a mile away from us.
> As the Stradivarius had thrown its most stirring melodies to the wind and waves the night before, we theorized that the cetacean was drawn to these unfamiliar sounds.
> A naturalist who was with us did not deny this, and from then on it was conventional wisdom onboard that whales, like turtles, were *dilettanti* of the highest order.

I wonder if Rothenberg (who was also on a boat with his instrument, but in active dialogue with the whales) felt as foreign when he listened to whale songs as I do looking at the codes of telecom technicians. The piece for clarinet and cetacean is beautiful, but don't you get the feeling that he's instrumentalizing—in every sense—the sounds of the whales? When I listen to "Valentine," I detect an urge to fill the silences. Or rather, that he's no longer allowing a connection between sound, silence, and space. In taking the whales' songs and joining them with his own, and by adding a studio backing track to the duet, he captures the whale songs in our human understanding of time and within the space of one piece of music. In doing so, does he not rupture the signifying temporality of their "units" of speech?

And even if there has been some interaction in the clarinet-whale duet (and why would emotions not flow both ways), who can say if the interaction was beneficial to them? In making anthropophony out of biophony, I am not sure that Rothenberg has created ecophony.

The ocean and its SOFAR channel, by which the lowest-pitched part of the whale song slowly traverses thousands of kilometers . . . The ocean and its submarine cable channels, by which all the world's data flits across thousands of kilometers at near light speed . . . Two parallel space-time universes.

And yet, the former is now under surveillance by the latter. Did you know that recently, dark fibers (meaning fibers that are no longer active) from submarine cables have been used to track whale songs in the ocean? The fiber-optic cable itself, acting like an interferometer, picks up the variations in pressure associated with waves spreading in water, whether they are caused by whale songs, the sound of a supercargo engine, or vibrations caused by an earthquake. An "interrogator" converts this mechanical momentum into electrical signals. Since optical fibers are sensitive to pressure changes caused by sound waves through their entire run, they have very high resolution and sensitivity. And since there are already 1.3 million kilometers of submarine cables in the ocean, there is enormous potential for Distributed Acoustic Sensing. Might this technique also document how whale songs are changing, even as digital infrastructure, which contributes to ocean warming, is itself one of the causes of vocal adaptation in underwater animals?

I wonder, too, if the fiber-optic cables that run together in the basement of my building could act like interferometers for the sounds of each floor. In addition to transmitting data, they'd also sense the pressures of voices, songs, cries, tears, and laughter from our neighbors. Listen—aren't those the signals of a voice, a voice reading *The Mahabharata*?

Casting our eyes on the great ocean extending over many hundreds of *Yojanas* and abounding in whales and alligators and other aquatic animals, we became anxious and filled with grief.

Have a good week!

Ariane

– Bruno Latour and Émilie Hermant, *Paris: Invisible City*, trans. Liz Carey-Libbrecht (virtual book, 2006), 27, http://www.bruno-latour.fr/sites/default/files/downloads/viii_paris-city-gb.pdf.
– Caspar Henderson, *A Book of Noises: Notes on the Auraculous* (University of Chicago Press, 2023).
– Lise Cristiani, "Voyage dans la Sibérie orientale, notes extraites de la correspondance d'une artiste (Mlle Lise Cristiani)," *Le tour du monde: Nouveau journal des voyages* (January 1863): 395.
– On tracking whales using fiber-optic cables, see Robin André Rørstadbotnen, "Simultaneous Tracking of Multiple Whales Using Two Fiber-Optic Cables in the Arctic," *Frontiers* 10 (2023), https://doi.org/10.3389/fmars.2023.1130898
– Excerpt from *The Mahabharata*, trans. Kisari Mohan Ganguli (Munshiram Manoharial, 1970), bk. 3, section CCLXXX.

[Monday, December 30, 2024]

My dear Ariane,

I hope you're having a nice vacation. Did you end up giving your English cousins the little music boxes that we talked about on the phone just before you left?

Believe it or not, I didn't know anything about the phenomenon of SOFAR. I find it fascinating that temperature, pressure, and salinity can transform a simple horizontal layer of seawater into a canal that slows down and prolongs sound. It's a bit like a machine that slows down time, isn't it? Have you read the papers? The whales haven't been the only ones under surveillance these last few weeks. The War of Cables has been declared. There were incidents in November in the Baltic Sea: infrastructure severed, entire regions disconnected, a Chinese ship is under suspicion. NATO has since announced that it detected a Russian ship the size of a large fishing trawler plying international waters. "It's following the exact path of our submarine cables!" disclosed a European military source to a major daily newspaper, in which I learned that the electromagnetic equipment on board the *Kildin*—that's its name—allows it to detect critical Western infrastructure by listening for it.

I took advantage of the Christmas break to listen to *Vox Balaenae* and *Whale Music* again. The two have essentially opposite approaches! Crumb listens to and is inspired by whale songs to compose his piece in eight movements for flute, cello, and piano, while Rothenberg flies all over the world, going out on boats to record whales using a hydrophone dropped in the water and playing *them* the clarinet through a microphone connected to an underwater loudspeaker. Does he really improvise with them, or is he just invading their silences, perhaps even muting them without even realizing it? You're quite right to raise the question.

Personally, I'm troubled by something else: his music is scrubbed of the sounds of all the infrastructure that made it possible. Gone is the thrum of the pre-amp, the lapping of the ocean against the hull of the boat, the clatter of the halyard on the mast! Rothenberg establishes the illusion of proximity, of a "natural" meeting with the cetacean, making the listener forget that the dinghy engine, the plane's landing gear on the tarmac in Honolulu, and the taxi radio on the way to the airport were all needed to enable this. I think our relationship with silence is quite ambiguous. On the one hand, we disapprove of silence, since it signals the disappearance of other people's songs and lives; on the other hand, we are constantly manufacturing it to avoid hearing our own technical metabolism.

I also went by 8 rue Lambert again. The Beast appeared to be sleeping. While you were lying in wait, before you heard its low-pitched buzzing and felt its whoosh of hot air, did you notice the portraits of Rimbaud and Verlaine on the house at the corner of rue Nicolet? I just learned that that's where they first met, on September 10, 1871. I wonder whether, on that evening, Arthur read to Paul the most sonorous quatrain from *Drunken Boat*?

Blanker than the brain of a child I fled
Through winter, I scoured the furious jolts of the tides,
In an uproar and a chaos of Peninsulas,
Exultant, from their moorings in triumph torn.

No more triumphant uproar and chaos at no. 8! As the lady told you, the commotion of the print shop was replaced by the silence of the server; by now you've no doubt guessed that this invisible, nearly mute space is connected underground to the wires I had you follow in your own building, Ariane. If you'd followed the Free cable into the sewers, you would have turned right under rue Ramey, then left under rue Bachelet directly beneath the whale fresco and the Palestinian poem, before turning right on rue Lambert. I doubt very much that you would have been able to get to the ground floor of no. 8 from below: it's a network node where all the fiber-optic lines in your neighborhood come together to connect to the global internet.

I've never managed to get inside, nor seen anyone enter. It was explained to me that there is an uninterruptible power supply, backup batteries, fiber-optic cables, a distribution frame, a network switch, and fiber-optic patch cables inside. All this equipment is ventilated by the slats of the façade, and regularly cooled by the air conditioning unit you heard on your second visit with Elsa.

In Paris, all such rooms that Free operates are camouflaged behind false storefronts so as not to be seen. I passed by the one on rue Lambert many times before I noticed it. In French technical jargon, this type of equipment is called a *nœud de répartition optique* (optical distribution node), since fibers are distributed from there toward customers' buildings and apartments. I see another form of optical distribution in this name, one that distributes what we do or don't want to see, know or not know. As you could tell, there is almost never anything to hear at 8 rue Lambert, which has been soundproofed and insulated. But it seems important to me to go and take a listen, as you did, in order to understand that every once in a while indoor IT equipment breathes, too. That's why I like to believe that the ground floor of 8 rue Lambert—like the ground floors of 17 rue Vauvenargues, 19 rue de Germain Pilon, 11 rue de Saint-Luc, 39 rue Pajol, and so on (there are more than seventy of them in the capital)—are inhabited by living beings who now belong to our ecosystem, and who breathe the same Paris air that we do.

Whales, too, only take a few seconds every hour to come to the surface and breathe before diving back down to the depths. Sailors can hope to see them and identify their species by the shape of the powerful jets of water they shoot out, which sound like cannonballs.

"In dealing with the whale, we wish to speak only to reason. And yet the imagination will be moved by the sheer size of the objects we will discuss," warns Étienne Lacépède at the beginning of his volume on Cetacea, an addition to *Buffon's Natural History*.

Did you know that the nostrils on the top of a cetacean's head are called *évents* (blowholes) in French? In old dictionaries, that also means "the uncovering of something that one wished to keep secret."

After quickly breathing in, the whales return to the abyss. If they can escape the whistle of sonar, the crack of thawing ice floes, and the grinding of ships laying cable, their songs might cross paths with my message wishing you a very happy New Year.

I'll be glad to accept your invitation for Sunday by the fire. I'll walk over, by way of rue Lambert.

Love,
Soline

– George Crumb, *Vox Balaenae* (1972).
– Julien Bouissou, "Avec le rachat de Quiet-Oceans par une filiale du CNES, la surveillance acoustique des océans prend une nouvelle dimension," *Le Monde,* December 31, 2024.
– Edmond Lepelletier, *Paul Verlaine: His Life—His Work*, trans. E. M. Lang (Duffield, 1909).
– Arthur Rimbaud, "Drunken Boat," in Samuel Beckett, *Collected Poems in English and French* (Grove, 1977), 95.
– Étienne de Lacépède, *Histoire naturelle des cétacées*, continuation of *Histoire naturelle, générale et particulière* by George-Louis Leclerc, comte de Buffon (Paris, 1804), 1.

Can You Hear the Swamp Sing?
A Sonic Walk Through Vienna's Wetlands

Julia Grillmayr, Christina Gruber & Sophia Rut
(Lobau Listening Comprehensions)

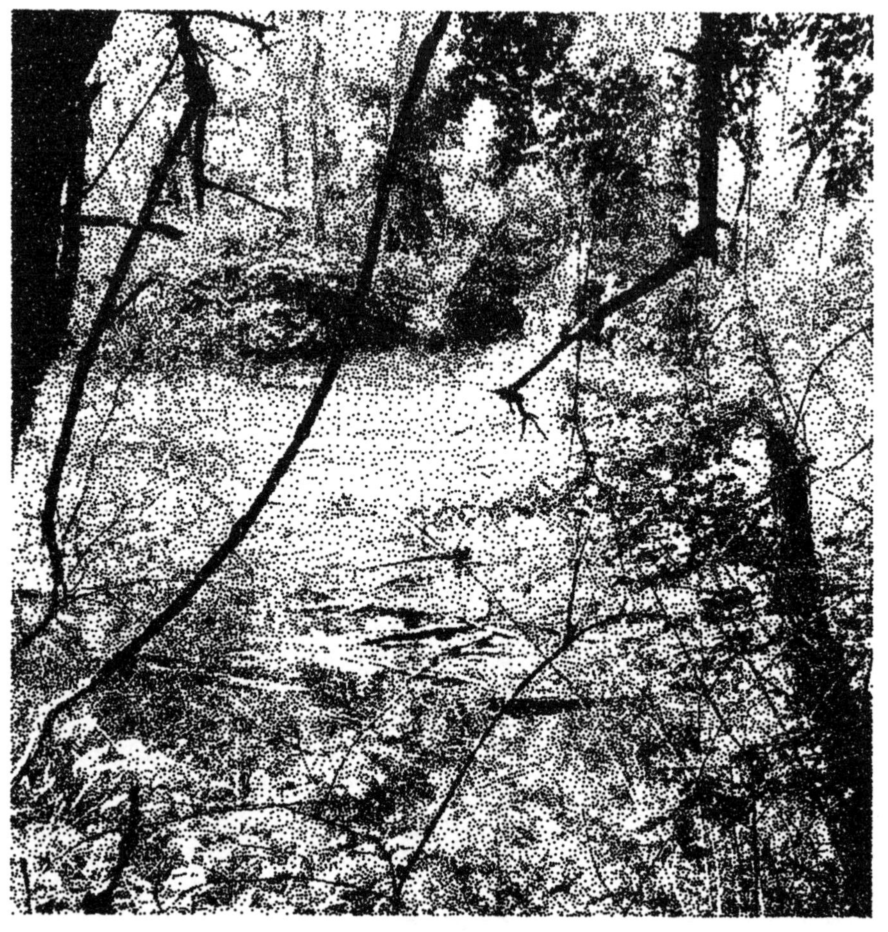

Field recording in Lobau, Julia Grillmayr

INTRODUCTION

Lobau Listening Comprehensions (LLC) emerged as a site-specific, acoustic investigation of the Lobau, Vienna's Danube floodplains. The LLC collective comprises cultural studies scholar and science journalist Julia Grillmayr, artist and freshwater ecologist Christina Gruber, and social ecology scholar and environmental historian Sophia Rut. For further information, please visit https://lobaulistening.at/.

WILDERNESS OF THE VIENNESE

I hear loud whooshing sounds; the clanging and clattering of metal, cars with trailers and some heavy trucks rushing by. I'm at one of the entries to the Donau-Auen National Park, the part we call Lobau.

"Our sound walk through the so-called 'Wilderness of the Viennese' starts here on 'Refinery Street.' On your right, you can see the 'Ölhafen Lobau,' the massive oil terminal."

I have a small loudspeaker with me on the tour, and I consider playing a recording I made several weeks ago. I bike here often and as a radio journalist and field recorder, I immediately had the impulse to stand still, take out my phone and press "record." The bike path that connects the upper and lower part of the national park leads past huge oil tanks, pipelines, and lots of machinery whose function I don't know. The last time I biked here, the whole infrastructure was singing, probably vibrating with chemicals and substances flowing through the pipelines and tubes. It was beautiful, alien and eerie. But my ears are already filled with industrial sounds, the trucks are rushing by loudly and a cargo train starts with its familiar heavy metal clatter. Psch psch psch.

"This train belongs to the Oil Terminal Trainline, which still exists. It will go on from here to the freight station Stadlau, transporting various commodities. The crude oil travels via pipeline to the refinery in Schwechat on the other side of the Danube."

Psch psch psch. The Danube River Basin is Europe's second largest river basin. In its Austrian section, the Danube is an Alpine river alternating her flow between narrow breakthrough stretches and vast basins where wide floodplain forests could form, leaving room for the river. In the late nineteenth century, these rich ecosystems were humanly modified, transforming the Austrian Danube into an industrialized river detached from its floodplains.

"What exactly is the Lobau?" "What we call Lobau surrounds us . . . it depends on how you define it. When we refer to Lobau, we often mean the Viennese part of Donau-Auen National Park. Even though we're standing next to an oil terminal, we're also very close to the entrance of the nature reserve, stretching from Vienna's eastern outskirts to the border with Slovakia. 'Lo-bau' means 'water forest.'" *Another car rushes by. I'm used to this loud, unpleasant sound, but, so close to the entrance of the national park, I feel the urge to escape and move on.*

Noise pollution was never part of the nature protection plans for the national park, so in addition to the fossil fuels running through the wetlands, the air above is heavily populated with aircraft descending and ascending at Austria's largest airport in Schwechat, Vienna International Airport.

"Let's leave Raffineriestrasse and move on! We're entering the national park at a gate called 'Lobgrundstrasse.' As we pass, we'll see the monument commemorating the forced labor camp the Nazis built here."

I wonder if our listening tour should begin with all this information about the troubled past of this place, but we can't avoid it—Lobau is full of it. Besides the oil terminal and the many bomb craters in the area that now gather water to form beautiful ponds, there's the Danube-Oder Canal, a planned waterway between the two rivers. This was an old dream of Roman emperors that the Nazis revived and partially built through the Lobau. Today, I swim in its wider sections, and in the narrower overgrown areas I watch turtles and butterflies. For me, despite its paradoxes, Lobau is a green refuge in stark contrast to the gray of the city.

LISTENING ABOVE AND BELOW

"Okay, here it's nice! This pond is called Panozzalacke. It was a former side arm of the meandering Danube, now cut off from the river by damming. Feel free to jump in!"

My son is only six months old, and he cheerfully greets every body of water we approach, starting by imitating gurgling sounds. For years, I've focused my work on the acoustic ecology of rivers and their inhabitants. Underwater microphones are my companions on every field trip I take, and today I'll also plunge the hydrophones into the Panozzalacke to listen.

"We are Christina Gruber, Sophia Rut, and Julia Grillmayr and as the Lobau Listening Comprehensions research collective, we undertake an acoustic exploration of the pasts, presents, and futures of this place. However, our projects are less about creating great field recordings and more about going to Lobau with you; to listen and record collectively in order to pay a different kind of attention. So, we're going to make recordings along our walk."

All my radio shows about the Lobau feature car noise in the form of an endless, homogeneous buzz. The walk participants already suspect as much. Still, after having to put walking and talking on pause because of the deafening noise of cars and trucks, I enter the national park almost ceremoniously and am greeted by the shrill cry of a bird in the reeds.

"As part of our artistic investigation of this place, we wanted to build a cyborg, an organic machine. A liminal entity in the in-between of tech- and biosphere we can cooperate with to describe this place through sound and audio recordings; a cyborg that could remix and play back the audio recordings we make. We called this entity GERTI."

I've come to sit in a meadow, which already hints at a different landscape, a dry grassland, called "Heisslände" or "Brenne." It is a bit counterintuitive, but these dry, hot, prairie-like ecosystems are also specific to Lobau and are highly biodiverse. The hum of insects is now omnipresent.

"We wanted to make a technical device to mediate these specific landscapes of Lobau and also to make it very clear that our "wetland listening" is not an immersion "in nature" or at least not merely that. We are constantly doing recordings with technical aids. We use technology to come here. A lot of infrastructure ensures that this place still exists in this form. We didn't want to present Lobau in our field recordings as a world without humans."

Children are laughing in the distance. Up close, gravel grinds as a bike passes by quickly. Also, the birds are getting louder all of a sudden. I swat at a mosquito that sucks blood from my arm. My children are chanting "Lobau bleibt! Lobau bleibt!"—a protest song they picked up at one of the regular demonstrations on Vienna's streets against the construction of a highway under the national park. This song is part of a rich history of protest connected to this place. The planned highway is just another of many threats in the history of this suburban landscape. In my work as an environmental historian and as a curator, I have conducted dozens of interviews with activists who were already campaigning half a century ago for the preservation of the Danubian floodplain forest and a different approach to our environment.

"In this process, we came to understand, that the Lobau itself is a technically transformed place and, of course, also a cultural place. We wanted to make this mixed situation visible or . . . audible. This many-layered history . . . We constantly encounter markers of political history in this landscape. Now, when we listen, we hear people swimming, insects chirping, the rustling of leaves, but we also hear the highway, the oil terminal train . . . all these things. When you're doing field recordings here, you can never pretend to be in a so-called wilderness even though you're standing in a floodplain forest, a national park." *Am I a river too? The heat of this summer day reveals my watery side, making me and the little human attached to me sweat to release some steam. After all, we are containers for water to move around in. This becomes even more evident while moving through this wetland, listening for the floodplain and its characteristic soundscape.*

"That's what interested us: How can we avoid concealing this and still build a meaningful relationship with the floodplain and its nonhuman inhabitants? How can we encounter this natural-cultural-technological-sociopolitical history cluster and still understand it as a species-rich and ecologically valuable space?"

VOICES OF THE SWAMP

Listening underwater is like taking a break from everything buzzing around us; it acts like a filter and a constant reminder that there is always this other world happening simultaneously underwater. It takes some time to attune to hear the subtle reverberations of aquatic plants swaying, the occasional splash of carp fish, the burbling of flowing streams, the distant calls of waterfowl, and, more prominently, the plunging sounds of children running into the water and diving down to the microphone, blubb-blublubb-blublubb.

"At first, we referred to GERTI as a cyborg, but then we realized that the Lobau itself is actually the cyborg, the organic machine. It's a being that is in between nature and culture. GERTI is an adapter to this landscape."

As a freshwater ecologist, I worship floodplains; here, borders become blurry, and everything is constantly transitioning. In ecology, these types of landscapes are called ecotones. In our case, we can only hear the remnants of them, but even so, this is truly magical.

"Here is a magic spot! This tree standing nearly in the water. I love this tree, which is actually two trees that have grown together at the base. It is a black poplar, a typical wetland tree. Now we're at Fasangartenarm ("Pheasant Garden Arm"). It's mostly fed by groundwater, but now more water is coming from the main stream, because of a new profile that cuts through the dyke and allows water to flow from the main arm of the Danube into the Lobau. This simulates the floodplain dynamics... to a certain extent. It's a mitigation measure to prevent the Lobau from drying up."

The shallow water and swamp forest vegetation provide habitat for frogs, ducks, and other birds, small warblers that jump between the reeds. I hear them more than I can see them. The group pauses, and the audio equipment is passed around. Everybody is quiet and listens to the many voices of the swamp.

"Who wants to take the microphone?"

Somebody hidden in the reeds emits a loud and intricate chirping sound. I glance at the group and realize that we are knowingly looking at each other and at the handheld recorders, satisfied to have captured this beautiful voice. But it is not only larger animals that are in our hearing range. It will be difficult to record this, but another central acoustic impression is the sound of mosquitoes humming as they come close to our ears. After all, this place is a wetland.

After several hours in the floodplains, we end our sonic swamp tour and begin moving back to the city. Evening has come, and with it, the mosquitoes. Our group slowly disperses. Some stay a bit longer at the pond, while others start walking back to the bus station where we started our tour. We all carry a bit of the Lobau with us, in the form of our collected recordings, but even more from having spent time together outside, listening. This embodied approach allows us to sense the rich biodiversity, the environmental history, and the ecological transformations still to come for the Viennese wetlands.

The Silent Academy

Yuri Tuma (Institute for Postnatural Studies)

The Silent Academy (SA) defines silence as a soundscape free from the memory of capitalist industrial noise. For most survivors of the Sonic Wars and the last events of the great aural crisis, this is a virtually unattainable acoustic space. The mission of the SA was based on one last hope: that the postwar generation could thrive in the renewal of the collective human spirit.

The philosophical pillar of the academy is rooted in the practice of deep listening, a way of being that guided civilization to prevail over the previous colonial oppression.[1] Unexpectedly, the Sonic Wars ended the long-lasting world order of deep listeners, who had managed to establish universal active listening, enabling a period of empathic interspecies coexistence. Despite their extensive training, they were unprepared for the technological evolution of sonic weapons developed by the opposition movement, the Lovelessness regime (formerly known as heteropatriarchy), which rejected listening as a means of belonging to the planetary collective and the cosmology of deep time. The acoustic destruction that ravaged the planet was unpredictable, causing the fall of a humanity: most of the planetary population was deafened to the point of nonexistence.

After the catastrophe, some of the survivors began to rebuild their lives, seeking refuge in abandoned urban ruins, now teeming with nonhuman life. In this headquarters of the SA, a quote can be found engraved on one of the walls, which withstood the fall of the devastated communities: "The search for love continued even in the face of great odds."[2] Since the academy's inauguration, it has symbolized one of the fundamental principles of the new academy: love is the basis of its transformational program, and it permeates and nourishes all the work developed in the five complete compostable programs.

This chapter of the SA is thriving in these latitudes of the island. Ours, meanwhile—located on the farthest northern shore—is struggling to mediate the differences between some of the individuals who are interfering with the safe sacred space and preventing frequency synchronizations in conflict resolutions. I was sent here to learn from the methodologies applied in its study program and was asked, in return, to formulate an unofficial manual.

After spending three water cycles here, I witnessed some of the methodologies that have guaranteed a continuous flow of harmonious disagreements based on collective care. Here, students of the Silent Academy receive carefully designed training in listening techniques and ways of being. They learn to pay attention to the subtle nuances of sonic frequencies, to distinguish between different rhythms and textures, and to allow these sounds to reverberate within their own emotional and biological states.

What follows are preliminary descriptions and instructions for some of the modules I was invited to participate in:

⚹. EMBODIED PSITHURISM

During one of their learning cycles, the students embody a tree and spend a season rooted in the earth, drinking only rainwater and finding their nutrients through sunlight. After this transformative curriculum of arboreal embodiment, they emerge with a deep understanding of the forest network. Their new sensitivity to sound extends not only to the auditory but also to the vibrational and energetic aspects of the island's biome. They actively listen to the symphony of their surroundings, thus learning the differences between sonic intrusion and auditory tuning with the environment, a practice more typical of certain birds, insects, or reptiles. As they rise from their rooted experience, the language of leaves and wind becomes their primary means of communication.

Instructions

Locate a spot within the forest where you feel a strong connection to the mycelial network. This may be a place where you sense a particular energy or a deep resonance with the trees. Press your ear gently against the soil to feel the vibrations of the earth. Excavate a small hole (approximately twenty-seven centimeters deep) using your hands. Place your feet firmly on the hole and then refill it with the soil you excavated. Engage the vertical support technology. When the sun is out, close your eyes and courageously repeat the *heliophilic affirmation* in your mind. Allow your awareness to shift from your brain to your feet, connecting with the energy of the root system of the trees around you. When it rains, remain grounded. Open your mouth and allow the rainwater inside of you. Once your thirst is satisfied, return your focus to the earth around your feet. Continue this process until you feel integration with the mycelial network and gently uproot yourself through gratitude.

HELIOPHILIC AFFIRMATION:

I surrender to your glow.
I am nourished by your fusion.
I am abundant in your light.

Some students are also given access to the songs of birds or other animal sounds, but the academy has no control over who is selected to receive this knowledge or why. Some are chosen seemingly at random, while others are drawn to the knowledge instinctively. A transcendental wisdom that allows them to intimately foster a sense of belonging with the nonhuman, the other-than-human, the more-than-human, and the other-than-animal. This element of chance and fate suggests that there is an invisible force guiding them.

Those who have access to these other modes of language guide the next learning cycle on interspecies communication. They lead others in an exploration of the expressive potential of the human voice, employing a wide range of vocal techniques and exercises to practice the emotional subtleties conveyed through nonverbal sounds. One of the ways they explore their vocal abilities is through the imitation of other animals. This methodology activates a genetic ancestral memory of the primal origin of the human voice. It allows individuals to explore the sounds and emotions that predate the constraints of structured language. On moonless nights, they disperse throughout the territory and evoke wild sounds that live deep within their being. Animal spirits help them in this sonic incarnation. Many of them return from these experiences unable to communicate for a time. Some never regain their humanity; they choose to remain in their animality and disappear from the campus. One student recalls seeing a former academic running with a pack of wolves in the distance—he swore that they were howling in perfect interspecies unison.

Instructions

On a moonless night, spread out across a designated territory, ensuring you are within auditory range of your peers but out of direct sight. Begin the *rewilding meditation*, focusing on your breath and allowing your mind to connect with the animal spirit within. As you enter your animal state, you may experience a range of emotions, from radical joy to radical fear. Embrace the heightened feelings, for they are part of the transformation. Pay close attention to the sounds around you. They will trigger you in a different way now. Listen with savage intent and let your intuition guide you in what you communicate and at what volume. Proudly evoke the potential of your voice. If and when words return to you, rejoin the group.

REWILDING MEDIATION

Begin by closing your eyes and take a few deep breaths.
Allow the sensation of the air to flow through you, dissolving
the boundaries between mind and body. Release the grip
of reason and allow your being to simply be.

Picture yourself without human features—no skin,
hair, or fingernails. How does it feel?
What is your essence beyond the physical form?
Visualize a nonhuman body that could sustain this essence.
What image of self have you generated?

Now, imagine you are in a lush forest with a large lake.
How do you move in this environment in this nonhuman form?
Do you glide effortlessly through the trees?
Leap from branch to branch?
Glow in and out of existence?
Feel the freedom and the discomfort of new body
(or bodiless) movements.

Eventually, you arrive at a crossroads.
Two paths diverge before you.
Take a moment to sense the energy of each path.
Choose the one that resonates most with you.

As you walk along your chosen path, listen intently
to the soundscape around you.
The rustling of leaves, the chirping of birds,
the distant call of an animal . . .
What other sounds can you hear?

The path leads you to a vast open field bathed
in the light of a star-filled sky.
Look up and contemplate the immensity of the cosmos.
Enjoy a sense of awe and wonder.
Now, draw imaginary lines between the stars,
forming a constellation in the shape of an animal.

What animal did you create?
Spend some time reflecting on this creature.
What does it symbolize to you?
How does it connect to your own spirit?
When you feel ready, evoke the first sound that wants to come out of
your body, and become one with your animal spirit.

Here, the voice is also explored through the practice of collective healing. Groups of SA apprentices gather in humming circles. They begin to hum at a low volume, almost imperceptible to the untrained ear. In the middle of the solar day, the volume of their voices rises to a communal shout. These moments of resonance are called medicinal frequency circles. After the sessions, those who were physically, mentally, or emotionally unwell feel completely recovered and revitalized.

Instructions

Form a gentle circle with the group, standing or sitting, with your shoulders lightly touching those of your neighbors. When the circle is complete, your frequency healer will begin humming. Each person should then begin to hum, harmonizing with the healer's tone. Listen deeply to the collective hum, allowing it to guide your own vocalizations. Experience the collective hum as it gradually builds, feeling the energy of the group. As the hum intensifies, it will evolve into an open-mouthed vocalization. When the collective sound reaches a crescendo, the group's voice will naturally engage in a communal scream. When you reach this threshold, release any sense of lack from your spirit and body, and take in the abundance that surrounds you. After the scream, remain in silence for a few moments, allowing the energy to subside. You may choose to hug others who consent or take yourself into healing solitude.

Underwater listening is another core practice at the academy. In the first compostable program, apprentices learn to submerge their minds, immersing themselves in the sounds of the ocean through deep meditation and synchronized breathwork. They develop a heightened and fluid awareness of the hydrosphere, learning to perceive the subtle shifts in pressure, temperature, and currents.

Those who master this initial stage progress to actual water classrooms, where they learn to echolocate, utilizing subtle shifts in their own vibrational frequency to sense their surroundings. This advanced form of perception creates a unique form of isolation. For while their awareness expands, their ability to communicate with those who haven't undergone this training diminishes. The untrained human, vibrating at a terrestrial frequency, becomes increasingly difficult to understand.

During the later stages of the training, dolphins begin to appear close to the shore, drawn to the unique vibrational signatures of the apprentices. These encounters lead to unexpected and profound connections, blurring the lines between human and cetacean consciousness. Aquatic relationships flourish for some of the most advanced underwater listeners, sometimes leading to profound interspecies love and even romantic bonds.

Instructions for initial stage

Find a rock formation with an active blowhole near the shore. Sit comfortably next to it, facing the ocean. Close your eyes and begin the *inner-sea meditation*, focusing on your breath, feeling the rhythmic currents of the waves. Inhale at the speed of the air that is expelled from the blowhole. Exhale at the speed of the air that recedes, allowing the rhythm of your breath to synchronize with the ocean's. Remain in this state of breath kinship until you feel a deep sense of interconnectedness with the microorganic life forms that reside within you.

INNER-SEA MEDITATION

Begin by grounding yourself, sensing the rock beneath you.
Close your eyes and take a few deep breaths.
Feel the sensation of the air flowing through you,
dissolving the boundaries between mind and body.

Allow your spirit to slowly walk toward the water.
As you approach the water's edge, notice the sound
of the waves gently lapping against the shore.

Now, imagine entering the water with gratitude
and submerging yourself completely.
Visualize your body dissolving into the water,
becoming one with the ocean.
A myriad of life-forms thrive within you.
What living organisms can you sense?
How do they move?
How do they communicate?
How do they play?
Listen to their sounds, observe their motions,
feel the flow of life all around you. Experience the liquid
joy of interconnectedness.

As you emerge from the water, carry this feeling with you,
and listen attentively to the waves.
As they rise, the water moves inland, and as they recede,
the water moves seaward. Synchronize your breath with
this movement and breathe with the ocean.

⋆. ᯓ °. MYCELLIC TELEPATHY

After a long period of learning, this is my last water cycle at this campus of the Silent Academy. The academic body will soon celebrate their Liquid Earth anniversary. During their ritual ceremony, they willingly take a mushroom that activates cosmological listening, transporting them on a transcendental aural journey. These auditory experiences allow them to communicate through telepathy, a form of exchange that also enables them to reverberate with their multiple identities, with their past and future lives. It will be the last experience I will share before my return and one of the most revealing of their radical practices. Once the fungal effect is over, we will walk in empathic silence for as long as our collective will lasts, and there we will sleep for several lunar cycles to complete the academy's curriculum in the classroom of dreams.

1 Inspired by Pauline Oliveros's practice of Deep Listening.

2 bell hooks, *All About Love* (Harper Perennial, 2001), xv.

Four Objections to the Concept of Soundscape

Tim Ingold

I very much welcome the recent growth of interest in sound, the impact of which is being felt not only in my own discipline of anthropology but also in the related fields of art, architecture, and archaeology, to name just a few. But I am also concerned lest we repeat mistakes that have already befallen studies in visual culture. The "visual," in these studies, appears to have little or nothing to do with what it means to be able to see. That is to say, it scarcely deals with the phenomenon of light. It is rather about the relations between objects, images, and their interpretations. A study of aural culture, built along the same lines, would be about the interpretation of a world of things rendered in their acoustic forms. It has become conventional to describe such a world by means of the concept of soundscape.[1] Undoubtedly when it was first introduced, the concept served a useful rhetorical purpose in drawing attention to a sensory register that had been neglected relative to sight. I believe, however, that it has now outlived its usefulness. More to the point, it carries the risk that we might lose touch with sound in just the same way that visual studies have lost touch with light. In what follows, I will set out four reasons why I think the concept of soundscape would be better abandoned.

First, the environment that we experience, know, and move around in is not sliced up along the lines of the sensory pathways by which we enter into it. The world we perceive is the *same* world, whatever path we take, and in perceiving it, each of us acts as an undivided center of movement and awareness. For this reason, I deplore the fashion for multiplying *scapes* of every possible kind. The power of the prototypical concept of landscape lies precisely in the fact that it is not tied to any specific sensory register—whether of vision, hearing, touch, taste, or smell. In ordinary perceptual practice these registers cooperate so closely, and with such overlap of function, that their respective contributions are impossible to tease apart. The landscape is of course *visible*, but it only becomes *visual* when it has been rendered by some technique, such as of painting or photography, which then allows it to be viewed indirectly, by way of the resulting image, which, as it were, returns the landscape back to the viewer in an artificially purified form, shorn of all other sensory dimensions. Likewise, a landscape may be *audible*, but to be *aural* it would have to have been first rendered by a technique of sound art or recording, such that it can be *played back* within an environment (such as a darkened room) in which we are otherwise deprived of sensory stimulus.[2]

We should not be fooled by art historians and other students of visual culture who write books about the history of seeing that are entirely about the contemplation of images. Their conceit is to imagine that the eyes are not so much organs of observation as instruments of playback, lodged in the image rather than the body of the observer. It is as though the eyes did our seeing for us, leaving us to (re)view the images they relay to our consciousness. For the active looking and watching that people do as they go about their business, visual theorists have substituted regimes of the "scopic," defined and distinguished by the recording and playback functions of these allegorical eyes. Although the apparent etymological kinship between the scopic and the "scapes" of our perception is spurious, such a connection is commonly presumed.[3] Thus, in resorting to the notion of soundscape, we run the risk of subjecting the ears, in studies of the aural, to the same fate as the eyes in visual studies. This is my second objection to the concept. We need to avoid the trap, analogous to thinking that the power of sight inheres in images, of supposing that the power of hearing inheres in recordings. For the ears, just like the eyes, are organs of observation, not instruments of playback. Just as we use our eyes to watch and look, so we use our ears to listen as we go forth in the world.

It is of course to light, and not to vision, that sound should be compared. The fact, however, that sound is so often and apparently unproblematically compared to *sight* rather than light reveals much about our implicit assumptions regarding vision and hearing, which rest on the curious idea that the eyes are screens that block out the light, leaving us to reconstruct the world inside our heads, whereas the ears are holes in the skull that let the sound in so that it can mingle with the soul.[4] One result of this idea is that the vast psychological literature on optical illusions is unmatched by anything on the deceptions of the ear. Another is that studies of visual perception have had virtually nothing to say about the phenomenon of light. It would be unfortunate if studies of auditory perception were to follow suit and to lose touch with sound, just as visual studies have lost touch with light. Far better, by placing the phenomenon of sound at the heart of our inquiries, we might be able to point to parallel ways in which light could be restored to the central place it deserves in understanding visual perception. To do this, however, we have first to address the awkward question: what *is* sound? This question is a version of the old philosophical conundrum: Does the tree falling in a storm make any sound if there is no creature present with ears to hear it? Does sound consist of mechanical vibrations in the medium? Or is it something we register only inside our heads? Is it a phenomenon of the material world or of the mind? Is it "out there" or "in here"? Can we dream it?

It seems to me that such questions are wrongly posed, in so far as they set up a rigid division between two worlds, of mind and matter—a division that is reproduced every time that appeal is made to the *materiality* of sound. Sound, in my view, is neither mental nor material, but a phenomenon of *experience*—that is, of our immersion in, and commingling with, the world in which we find ourselves. Such immersion, as the philosopher Maurice Merleau-Ponty insisted, is an existential precondition for the isolation both of minds to perceive and of things in the world to be perceived.[5] To put it another way, just as light is another way of saying, "I can see," so is sound another way of saying "I can hear."[6] If this is so, then neither sound nor light, strictly speaking, can be an *object* of our perception. Sound is not *what* we hear, any more than light is what we see. Herein lies my third objection to the concept of soundscape. It does not make sense for the same reason that a concept of "lightscape" would not make sense.[7] The scaping of things—that is, their surface conformation—is revealed to us thanks to their illumination. When we look around on a fine day, we see a landscape bathed in sunlight, not a lightscape. Likewise, listening to our surroundings, we do not hear a soundscape. For sound, I would argue, is not the object but the medium of our perception. It is what we hear *in*. Similarly, we do not see light but see *in* it.[8]

Once light and sound are understood in these terms, it becomes immediately apparent that in our ordinary experience, the two are so closely involved with one another as to be virtually inseparable. This involvement, however, raises interesting questions that we are only beginning to address. How, for example, does the contrast between light and darkness compare with that between sound and silence? It is fairly obvious that the experience of sound is quite different in the dark than in the light. Does the experience of light likewise depend on whether we are simultaneously drowned in sound or cocooned in silence? These kinds of questions bring me to my fourth objection to the concept of soundscape. Since it is modelled on the concept of landscape, soundscape places the emphasis on the *surfaces* of the world in which we live. Sound and light, however, are infusions of the *medium* in which we find our being and through which we move. Traditionally, both in my own discipline of anthropology and more widely in fields such as cultural geography, art history, and material culture studies, scholars have focused on the fixities of surface conformation rather than the fluxes of the medium. They have, in other words, imagined a world of persons and objects that has already precipitated out, or solidified, from these fluxes.[9] Going on to equate the solidity of things with their materiality, they have contrived to dematerialize the medium in which they are primordially immersed. Even the air we breathe, and on which life depends, becomes a figment of the imagination.

Now the mundane term for what I have called the fluxes of the medium is *weather*. So long as we are—as we say—"out in the open," the weather is no mere phantasm, the stuff of dreams. It is, to the contrary, fundamental to perception. We do not perceive it; we perceive *in* it.[10] We do not touch the wind, but touch in it; we do not see sunshine, but see in it; we do not hear rain, but hear in it. Thus wind, sunshine and rain, experienced as feeling, light, and sound, are essential to our capacities, respectively, to touch, to see, and to hear.[11] In order to understand the phenomenon of sound (as indeed those of light and feeling), we should therefore turn our attention skywards, to the realm of the birds, rather than toward the solid earth beneath our feet. The sky is not an object of perception, any more than sound is.[12] It is not a thing we see. It is rather luminosity itself. But it is sonority too. Recall the argument of the musicologist Victor Zuckerkandl, that if we really want to know what it means to hear, we should gaze into the sky.[13] If he is right, then perhaps our metaphors for describing auditory space should be derived not from landscape studies but from meteorology.

Let me conclude with a couple of points that address not the concept of soundscape itself but rather its implied emphasis on, first, *embodiment*, and second, *emplacement*. I have mentioned the wind, and the fact that to live we must be able to breathe. Wind and breath are intimately related in the continuous movement of inhalation and exhalation that is fundamental to life and being. Inhalation is wind becoming breath, exhalation is breath becoming wind. At a recent anthropological conference on *Wind, Life, Health*, the issue came up of how the wind is embodied in the constitution of persons affected by it.[14] For my part, I felt uneasy about applying the concept of embodiment in this context. It made breathing seem like a process of coagulation, in which air was somehow sedimented into the body as it solidified. Acknowledging that the living body, as it breathes, is necessarily swept up in the currents of the medium, I suggested that the wind is not so much embodied as the body *enwinded.*[15] It seems to me, moreover, that what applies to wind also applies to sound. After all, the wind whistles, and people hum or murmur as they breathe. Sound, like breath, is experienced as a movement of coming and going, inspiration and expiration. If that is so, then we should say of the body, as it sings, hums, whistles, or speaks, that it is *ensounded.* It is like setting sail, launching the body *into* sound like a boat on the waves or, perhaps more appropriately, like a kite in the sky.

Finally, if sound is like the wind, then it will not stay put, nor does it put persons or things in their place. Sound flows, as wind blows, along irregular, winding paths, and the places it describes are like eddies, formed by a circular movement *around* rather than a fixed location *within.* To follow sound—that is, to *listen*—is to wander the same paths. Attentive listening, as opposed to passive hearing, surely entails the very opposite of emplacement. Again, the analogy with flying a kite is apposite. Though the flyer's feet may be firmly planted on the spot, it is not the wind that keeps them there. Likewise, the sweep of sound continually endeavors to tear listeners away, causing them to surrender to its movement. It requires an effort to stay in place. And this effort pulls *against* sound rather than harmonizing *with* it. Place confinement, in short, is a form of deafness.

[Reproduced from Tim Ingold, *Being Alive: Essays on Movement, Knowledge and Description* (Routledge, 2011), © Tim Ingold, 2011, reproduced by arrangement with Taylor & Francis Group]

NOTES

1 The concept of soundscape was introduced by the Canadian composer R. Murray Schafer in 1994 and has since been widely adopted. See R. Murray Schafer, *The Soundscape: Our Sonic Environment and the Tuning of the World* (Destiny Books, 1994).

2 One of the main ways in which a landscape is audible is in running water. "Streams and rivers," as Gaston Bachelard has pointed out, "provide the sound for mute country landscapes, and do it with a strange fidelity." Gaston Bachelard, *Water and Dreams: An Essay on the Imagination of Matter*, trans. Edith R. Farrell (Pegasus Foundation, 1983), 15.

3 See Tim Ingold, "Landscape or Weather-World?," in *Being Alive: Essays on Movement, Knowledge and Description* (Taylor & Francis, 2011).

4 See Tim Ingold, "Landscape or Weather-World?," 128.

5 Maurice Merleau-Ponty, "Eye and Mind," trans. Carleton Dallery, in *The Primacy of Perception: And Other Essays on Phenomenological Psychology, the Philosophy of Art, History and Politics*, ed. James M. Edie (Northwestern University Press, 1964).

6 Tim Ingold, "Landscape or Weather-World?," 128.

7 Mikkel Bille and Tim Flohr Sørensen have recently proposed an argument in support of the concept of lightscape. It is an argument, however, that proceeds by treating light not as a phenomenon of lived experience but as an object endowed with agency. See Mikkel Bille and Tim Flohr Sørensen, "An Anthropology of Luminosity: The Agency of Light," *Journal of Material Culture* 12, no. 3 (2007).

8 Tim Ingold, *The Perception of the Environment: Essays on Livelihood, Dwelling and Skill* (Routledge, 2000), 265.

9 See Tim Ingold, "Materials Against Materiality," in *Being Alive*, 26.

10 See Tim Ingold, "The Eye of the Storm: Visual Perception and the Weather," *Visual Studies* 20, no. 2 (2005).

11 See Ingold, "Landscape or Weather-World?," 130.

12 See Ingold, "Landscape or Weather-World?"

13 Victor Zuckerkandl, *Sound and Symbol: Music and the External World*, trans. Willard R. Trask, Bollingen Series 44 (Princeton University Press, 1956), 344.

14 Elisabeth Hsu and Chris Low, eds., *Wind, Life, Health: Anthropological and Historical Perspectives* (Blackwell, 2008).

15 Tim Ingold, "Earth, Sky, Wind and Weather," *Journal of the Royal Anthropological Institute* 13, no. s1 (April 2007): S32.

If Nothing Was Nothing How Could We Name It

Laura Vazquez, translated by Cole Swensen

On the sonic walk, a calm appears.
Animals, gestures, and time.
Attention is focused on something other than yourself or your own thoughts.
Then phrases come.
There is light and beings live.
These poems were inspired by this sonic walk.
Somewhere: they were drawn from it.

.I.

the sun is an element
the sun is an element
and the sun as well
as the sun is alone
the sun is an element
setting among the world
the sun among the world setting
on the people the sun setting on itself
on the people so the sun setting on the people is an element
the sun sets
on the people an element of the world

I lie down and so I lie down
I lie down on the people that I meet I am heavy
I am heavy
I lie down on you because I want to reach you I met
eyes voices and small insects and I lie down
I lie down on you in my mind I think
I think about you in my mind I think
the sun as well
when I love as well as the sun
as well as the people
when I love a person as such I stretch out
you must crush people
it's cold you must
you must crush people to understand
you must fall you must crush animals plants rocks
while the sun sets
the sun sets because it is
the sun sets because it is heavy
it is
the sun is alone
the sun is alone
but it doesn't know loneliness
but it doesn't know loneliness
the sun is an element among others
doesn't know loneliness
it doesn't know loneliness
no one knows loneliness
our bodies
a body doesn't know loneliness
no one
it doesn't know loneliness be it alone
be it alone
the sun was there when I was born
the sun beats down on the animals on the road the sun beats down
on animals thank you

.II.

I transform the faces of babies says the sun
I swallow the faces of newborns I'm at ease says the sun
and the sun meets the dead skin every bit of the outline
a particle of sunlight feels
for the sun
the particle of sunlight occurs for no reason
reason is an occurrence of the sun
the sun comes every morning into my black building
the sun comes
every morning my fixed face
the sun opens my eyes in my building the thoughts are made by the sun
in my apartment meetings within me are made
in a black building
the sun moves the thoughts inside
beings heat and light are movements within the being
babies or dead skin but beings of the sun's movements
are a kindness an innocence
light is an innocence a kindness an innocence

.III.

the sun is a science of life and the death of people and insects
the people are an abstraction so the sun explodes
I have the sun inside me but the sun explodes
to please evil
the sun will explode to please time and the line of facts
I took the wrinkles from my phrase to form the following
wrinkles not fear
wrinkles ask the sun to fold the body
of the sun is black wrinkle black
while the sun put wrinkles on people
while night fell the people shone in the night because of the sun
the people carried the sun through the night this woman has only calm wrinkles
these wrinkles sense everything's past certain thoughts wrinkle the dead
it happens to be a science a hand it happens to be a story of something real

Contributors

Valentin Bansac is an architect, researcher, and photographer from France. He previously worked with Rem Koolhaas at OMA/AMO, where he was part of *Countryside, The Future*, a research and exhibition project at Guggenheim New York. Valentin graduated from the Experimentation in Arts and Politics master's degree directed by Bruno Latour at the Paris Institute of Political Studies (Sciences Po). He was involved in the two-year research program Domesticated Foodscapes at ÉPFL (École Polytechnique Fédérale de Lausanne) and recently participated in Organismo | Art in Applied Critical Ecologies, an initiative facilitated by TBA21 Thyssen-Bornemisza Art Contemporary, an international art and advocacy foundation based in Madrid. In 2022, he co-founded the collective MATTERS.xyz, with Alice Loumeau, and co-curated the exhibition *Rire sur un volcan* at POUSH in Aubervilliers, France (January–March 2025).

Mike Fritsch is a Luxembourgish architect, urbanist, and educator working between Luxembourg and France. After having spent several years at OMA in Rotterdam, Mike oscillates, as a practicing architect, between large-scale transformation strategies and architectural repairs, both as an independent and in collaboration with l'AUC. In parallel, Mike is teaching at ÉNSA-Marseille, where he manipulates new territorial narratives on adaptations and social interactions of the "already there."

Alice Loumeau is a French Canadian architect, curator, and independent researcher. She conducts spatial investigations through writing and cartography, exploring the political and ecological controversies within mutating territories of the Anthropocene. Alice graduated from the Experimentation in Arts and Politics master's degree directed by Bruno Latour at the Paris Institute of Political Studies (Sciences Po) in 2022. Alice has worked as an architect at OMA/AMO in Rotterdam, at l'AUC and UR in Paris, and at Matheson Whiteley in London. She is involved in exhibitions, publications, and residencies, including at Villa Albertine in Marfa, Texas, in 2024. In 2022, she co-founded the collective MATTERS.xyz, with Valentin Bansac, and co-curated the exhibition *Rire sur un volcan* at POUSH in Aubervilliers, France (January–March 2025).

Peter Szendy is Professor of Humanities and Comparative Literature at Brown University and musicological advisor for the book series published by La Philharmonie de Paris. His publications include: *Powers of Reading: From Plato to Audiobooks* (Zone Books, 2025); *For an Ecology of Images* (Verso, 2025); *Bendings: Four Variations on Anri Sala* (Mudam-Mousse Publishing, 2019); *The Supermarket of the Visible: Toward a General Economy of Images* (Fordham University Press, 2019); *Of Stigmatology: Punctuation as Experience* (Fordham University Press, 2018); *All Ears: The Aesthetics of Espionage* (Fordham University Press, 2007); *Listen: A History of Our Ears* (Fordham University Press, 2001). He curated the exhibition *The Supermarket of Ima*ges at the Jeu de Paume museum in Paris (February–June 2020).

David George Haskell is a writer and a biologist. His latest book, *Sounds Wild and Broken* (Faber & Faber, 2022), was a finalist for the Pulitzer Prize for General Nonfiction and for the PEN / E. O. Wilson Literary Science Writing Award and winner of the Acoustical Society of America's Science Communication Award. His previous books, *The Forest Unseen* (Viking Books, 2012) and *The Songs of Trees* (Penguin Random House, 2017), have been acclaimed for their lyrical writing and rich attention to the living world. They have received various honors: finalist for the Pulitzer Prize for General Nonfiction, for the National Academies' Best Book Award, for the John Burroughs Medal, for the Iris Book Award, for the Reed Environmental Writing Award, and for the National Outdoor Book Award for Natural History Literature; and the Award in Literature from the American Academy of Arts and Letters.

He has also written essays and multimedia projects for *Emergence Magazine*, *The New York Times*, and other publications. He lives in Atlanta, Georgia, USA.

The **Bogong Centre for Sound Culture (B-CSC)** is an Australian arts initiative exploring the intersections of sound, ecology, and interdisciplinary practice. Located in the alpine environment of Bogong Village, Victoria, it provides artists and researchers with a unique setting for site-responsive projects. Founded in 2010 by Philip Samartzis and Madelynne Cornish, the B-CSC fosters creative inquiry through residencies, publications, and public programs. Its projects investigate environmental and industrial processes, using fieldwork, spatial sound, and experimental media to examine mutable landscapes and human impact. The B-CSC frequently engages with themes of climate change, land use, and ecological dissonance, highlighting overlooked aspects of the alpine environment. By facilitating collaboration across disciplines, the B-CSC cultivates innovative artistic and scholarly responses to place, expanding our understanding of the natural world through deep listening, critical reflection, and interdisciplinary dialogue.

Xabi Molia was born in the Basque Country in 1977. His first novel, *Fourbi* (Gallimard, 2000), was published while he was still a student. After earning a doctorate in film history, he taught at university until 2012, before devoting himself entirely to his dual career as a writer and filmmaker. The author of three feature-length fiction films and two documentaries (co-directed with his sister Agnès), he has published seven novels, including *Les premiers: Une histoire des super-héros français* (Le Seuil, 2017) and *Des jours sauvages* (Le Seuil, 2020). In August 2024, he published *La vie ou presque* (Le Seuil).

Emma McCormick Goodhart is an artist, writer, researcher, and dramaturge, who experiments across media, timescales, and modes of practice. Staged as soft architectures, social ecologies, and climate fictions, often more haptic than optic, her work attempts to retune the spaces that host it. Interested in how the elasticities of timescale help expand notions of "remote" sensing and long-distance listening, her case study for e-flux *Architecture of Lascaux IV*, a digital and sensory facsimile that enables us to hear through 25,000-year-old sound, formed the basis for a moonmilk-derived "scent climate" in *Hollow Earth: Art, Caves & The Subterranean Imaginary* at Nottingham Contemporary, UK. A first edition of the scent will launch in 2025. Her neon sign-sculpture, *glai glaai*, renders a subtle Thai-language homonym—ใกล้ (*glai*, or near) on one side, and ไกล (*glaai*, or far) on the other—and was recently installed across three floors of Bangkok Kunsthalle (Thailand) in connection with her artist residency in 2024.

Ludwig Berger is a German sound artist, musician, and educator, whose work explores the sonic presences of organisms and places. He focuses on interspecies, geological, and architectural listening in landscapes, paying particular attention to microscopic sounds such as insect communication, plant rhythms, and glacial melting. Through installations, compositions, and performances, he uncovers hidden processes and nonhuman perspectives in various environments. Trained in electroacoustic composition, he was a researcher at the Institute of Landscape Architecture at ETH Zurich and is a certified Deep Listening instructor. His practice integrates field recording, scientific inquiry, and speculative listening across disciplines. His work has received recognition from Prix Ars Electronica, the Sound of the Year Awards, and A Closer Listen's Best Soundscape Albums of the Decade. Raised in a village in the Palatinate Forest–North Vosges Biosphere Reserve (Germany/France), he is now based in Montreal.

Shannon Mattern is the Presidential Penn Compact Professor of Media Studies and the History of Art at the University of Pennsylvania. Before coming to Penn, she worked, between 2004 and 2022, in the School of Media Studies and the Department of Anthropology at The New School and collaborated regularly with the Parsons School of Design. She won The New School's Distinguished University Teaching Award. Her writing and teaching focus on archives, libraries, and other media spaces; media infrastructures; sites where data intersects with art and design; and media that shape our sensory experiences. She is the author of *The New Downtown Library: Designing with Communities* (2007); *Deep Mapping the Media City* (2015); *Code and Clay, Data and Dirt: 5000 Years of Urban Media* (2017), all published by University of Minnesota Press; and *A City Is Not a Computer* (Princeton University Press, 2021). She also contributes a regular long-form column about urban data and mediated infrastructures to *Places Journal*. In addition, she serves as president of the board of the Metropolitan New York Library Council and regularly collaborates on public design and interactive projects and exhibitions.

Nadine Schütz is a Swiss artist, composer, and sound architect based in Paris. She explores the auditory landscape as a living, creative score that informs and guides its own transformation. Her installations, performances, and acoustic designs interweave space and listening, nature and music, the urban and the (non)human. Through sound, she gives a voice to the environment, revealing its hidden dimensions and resonances. She holds a PhD in landscape acoustics from ETH Zurich, where she played a key role in founding the AudioVisual Lab, and pioneered the integration of listening practice and sound spatialization into landscape and urban design. She is an associate composer at IRCAM-STMS at Centre Pompidou Paris and a lecturer at ETH Zurich. Her works have been presented internationally, from Zurich and Paris to London, New York, Kyoto, Moscow, Naples, and Venice, shaping new ways of perceiving and experiencing sound in space.

Cole Swensen has published twenty collections of poetry, most recently *And, And, And* (Shearsman Books, 2023), which was long-listed for the Griffin Prize, and a volume of critical essays, *Noise That Stays Noise* (University of Michigan Press, 2011). Ten of her books have been translated into French (four with Éditions Corti), with others in Italian and Spanish. A former Guggenheim Fellow, she has won the Iowa Poetry Prize, the SF State Poetry Center Book Award, and the National Poetry Series and has been a finalist for the National Book Award and the LA Times Book Award. Also a translator, she has won the PEN USA Award in Translation, the 2024 ALTA National Translation Award, and the 2025 Stephen Mitchell Translation Prize. She divides her time between Paris and the San Francisco Bay Area.

Laure Brayer holds a PhD in architecture, is a researcher at the AAU-CRESSON laboratory (Ambiances, Architectures, Urbanities joint research unit), and teaches at ÉNSA Grenoble (Université Grenoble Alpes) on representational arts and techniques. Her research is focused on the sensory experiences of contemporary spatial transformations and on their manifold representations. Through in situ studies with local residents, her work interrogates the connection between mediation, criticism, and project, focusing on the creation of intermediate objects (sensory maps, transects, films, multimedia exhibitions) that enable storytelling about places and put practices and projects up for debate. Together with Olivier Labussière, she runs the Video Workshop.

Soline Nivet is an architect. She is also trained in the techniques and writing of radio and film documentaries. She listens, from an architectural perspective, to the world as it is created, built, repaired, or dismantled. As full professor and director of research at the Architecture Culture Société laboratory of ÉNSA Paris-Malaquais (PSL University), she directs the seminar Architectural Investigations, Scenes, Documents, Research. Whether in the form of documentary creations, exhibitions, books, or research articles, her work primarily questions the place and role of architecture in the social and cultural history of the Paris region.

Ariane Wilson trained as a historian, architect, and musician; she is an associate professor at ÉNSA Paris-Malaquais (PSL University). Ever since establishing her practice and publishing *Un violoncelle sur le toit du monde* (Presses de la Renaissance, 2002), she has favored walking as a method, in both her teaching and her personal investigations, coupled with listening—with the naked ear or augmented by her cello—as a means to intensify the spatial perception of the temporalities, materiality, and invisible vibrations of cities and landscapes. She has worked on a pedagogy of listening for students in architecture and edited *Sound Worlds from the Body to the City: Listen!* (Cambridge Scholars Publishing, 2019). She is currently exploring territories at the margins of the Île-de-France regional transport system in her studio Navigoland et Hors-Forfait, as well as triple border points.

Lobau Listening Comprehensions (LLC) is an acoustic investigation of the Vienna Danube floodplains—the Lobau. The LLC collective comprises cultural studies scholar and science journalist Julia Grillmayr, artist and freshwater ecologist Christina Gruber, and social ecology scholar and environmental oral historian Sophia Rut. In LLC, they bring together their respective work with audio recordings and listening practices, thus merging formerly separate goals and methodologies. The site-specific project emerged in 2023 at the University of Applied Arts Vienna and has continued to transform in various ways ever since.

Yuri Tuma is a Brazilian interdisciplinary artist based in Madrid working at the intersections of sonic ecologies, queer theory, and collective healing. His research centers on contemporary ecological narratives, active listening methodologies, and performance and sound art.

In early 2020, he co-founded the Institute for Postnatural Studies (IPS), a Spain-based platform dedicated to critical research, radical education, and contemporary cultural production that harnesses ecology, the arts, and design for the purposes of social transformation. Beyond his work with the IPS, Tuma exhibits internationally and has participated in residencies and pedagogical initiatives at a variety of institutions, including the Museo Nacional Centro de Arte Reina Sofía, Matadero, La Casa Encendida, INLAND, School of Commons, Galeria Municipal do Porto, and the Berlinale.

Tim Ingold is Emeritus Professor of Social Anthropology at the University of Aberdeen, UK, and a Fellow of the British Academy and the Royal Society of Edinburgh. He is author of *The Perception of the Environment* (Routledge, 2000), *Lines: A Brief History* (Routledge, 2016), and other works. He has spent twenty-five years at the University of Manchester, where he was appointed Max Gluckman Professor of Social Anthropology in 1995. A key aspect of Ingold's work continues to lie in his critical exploration of the links between environmental perception and skilled practice. In this, he has aimed to replace traditional models of genetic and cultural transmission with a relational approach focusing on the growth of embodied skills of perception and action within social and environmental contexts of development. Since 2002, most of Ingold's work has been situated at the interface between anthropology, art, and architecture.

Laura Vazquez is a poet and novelist. In 2023, she was awarded the Prix Goncourt for poetry for her body of work. In 2021, her novel *La semaine perpétuelle* (Sous-Sol, 2021) received a special mention from the Prix Wepler and the Prix de la page 111. In 2014, she received the Prix de la Vocation for her book *La main de la main* (Cheyne, 2014). Her poems have been translated into Arabic, Chinese, Dutch, English, German, Italian, Norwegian, Portuguese, Romanian, and Spanish. A resident of the Villa Medici in Rome for 2023, Laura regularly gives public readings of her texts around the world in settings that include the Ming Contemporary Art Museum, Shanghai (China), Centre Pompidou (Paris), Musée d'art contemporain de Genève (Switzerland), Norsk Litteraturfestival (Norway), Festival Voix Vives de Tolède (Spain), and Amsterdam Perdu Art Center (Netherlands). She regularly collaborates with artists such as Rebeka Warrior, Lorraine de Sagazan, Philippe Quesne, and Sivan Eldar and also runs weekly online writing workshops. She is co-editor of the magazine *Muscle* with Roxana Hashemi.

Editors:
Valentin Bansac, Mike Fritsch,
Alice Loumeau, Peter Szendy

Visual identity:
Pierre Vanni

Layout:
Noémie Santos, Pierre Vanni

Photography:
Valentin Bansac

Translations:
Benjamin Connor, Simon Horn,
Cole Swensen

Copyediting:
Simon Cowper

Proofreading:
Simon Cowper

Image correction:
ScanColor Reprostudio GmbH, Leipzig

Printing and binding:
Druckhaus Sportflieger, Berlin

Published by:
Spector Books
Harkortstraße 10
04107 Leipzig
www.spectorbooks.com
and
Kultur | lx – Arts Council Luxembourg
4 Bd Roosevelt
L-2450 Luxembourg
www.kulturlx.lu

Distribution:
Germany, Austria: GVA, Gemeinsame
Verlagsauslieferung Göttingen GmbH&Co.
KG, www.gva-verlage.de
Switzerland: AVA Verlagsauslieferung AG,
www.ava.ch
France, Belgium: Interart Paris,
www.interart.fr
UK: Central Books Ltd,
www.centralbooks.com
USA, Canada, Central and South America,
Africa: ARTBOOK/ D.A.P.,
www.artbook.com
Japan: twelvebooks,
www.twelve-books.com
South Korea: The Book Society,
www.thebooksociety.org
Australia, New Zealand:
Perimeter Distribution,
www.perimeterdistribution.com

This publication has been developed as part of the exhibition of the Luxembourg Pavilion at the 19th International Architecture Exhibition – La Biennale di Venezia:

Sonic Investigations

Curators:
Valentin Bansac, Mike Fritsch,
Alice Loumeau
With: Ludwig Berger, Peter Szendy

Commissioners:
Kultur | lx – Arts Council Luxembourg and LUCA – Luxembourg Center for Architecture, on behalf of the Luxembourg Ministry of Culture

With the kind support of:
Centre national de l'audiovisuel (CNA), Luxembourg
Luxembourg Embassy in Rome

Musée national d'histoire naturelle, Luxembourg
University of Luxembourg (Regenerative Social-Ecological Systems, Geography and Spatial Planning)
Nature and Forest Agency (ANF)
Enovos
SEO
SES (Société Européenne des Satellites)
LuxConnect
POLYTEC
Radioamateurs du Luxembourg
Pauline Oliveros Trust and Daniel Weintraub

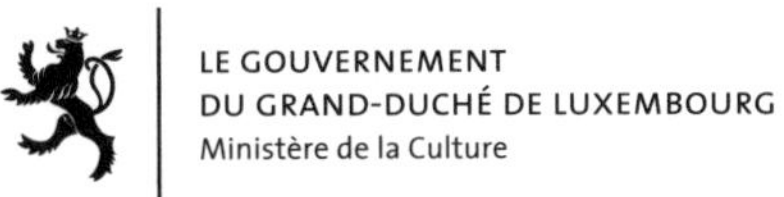

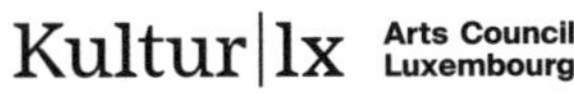

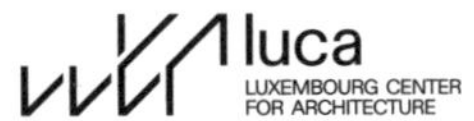

We thank the team of the exhibition of the Luxembourg Pavilion at the 19th International Architecture Exhibition – La Biennale di Venezia, entitled *Sonic Investigations:* Ludwig Berger, Peter Szendy, Pierre Vanni, and Anthea Caddy. We could not be more grateful for our collaboration and friendship.

Thanks to Joël Brücher, Emilie Gouleme, Pamela Medina Lopez, Eléonore Mialonier, Valérie Quilez, and Diane Tobes from Kultur | lx – Arts Council Luxembourg and Maribel Casas from LUCA – Luxembourg Center for Architecture.

Thanks to Marija Marić for her astute help.

Thanks to Michelle Friederici, Claudine Hemmer, Marion Waller, and Nemanja Zimonjić, who were part of the jury during the selection of the project.

Thanks to Andrea Mancini and Joel Valabrega as well as Alessandro Cugola, Martina Genovesi, Caterina Malavolti, and Juliane Seehawer from Every Island for their insights.

Thanks to Anne König and Jan Wenzel from Spector Books for making this book possible, and to Pierre Vanni and Noémie Santos for their work on the visual identity and layout.

Thanks to the authors, David George Haskell, Madelynne Cornish and Philip Samartzis (Bogong Centre for Sound Culture), Xabi Molia, Peter Szendy, Emma McCormick Goodhart, Ludwig Berger, Shannon Mattern, Nadine Schütz, Cole Swensen, Laure Brayer (AAU-CRESSON), Soline Nivet and Ariane Wilson, Julia Grillmayr, Christina Gruber and Sophia Rut (Lobau Listening Comprehensions), Yuri Tuma (Institute for Postnatural Studies), Tim Ingold, Laura Vazquez, and the translators Benjamin Connor and Simon Horn. Thanks to Simon Cowper for the copyediting and proofreading.

For *Sonic Investigations*, we thank Leonardo Bucalossi, Francesca Cau, Lisa Delmas, Tiphaine Marquet, and Renaud Sabari from ARTER.

Thanks to Roberto Barcaro and Thibault Verdron, as well as Fabio Botta and Maurizio Pessato from A.S. Italgroup.

Thanks to Alfonso Cabello, Vassia Gkogkou, Amanda Kelly, and Caroline Widmer from Pickles PR and to Nadia Fatnassi from Close Encounters.

Thanks to Hélène Kaizer, Philippe Mergen, Yves Steichen, and Gilles Zeimet from the Centre national de l'audiovisuel (CNA), Luxembourg, for their support.

Thanks to the Musée national d'histoire naturelle, Luxembourg, especially Paul Braun, Axel Hochkirch, Patrick Michaely, and Alexander Weigand, who helped identify species.
Thanks to Jacques Pir for the bats.

Thanks to the University of Luxembourg, especially Ariane König, Sophie Zuang, and Constance Carr for their specialist knowledge. Thanks to Martine Neuberg from the Nature and Forest Agency (ANF).

Thanks to Yann Arzani and Laurent Magi from Enovos.

Thanks to Olivier Felgen, Steve Heirens and Luc Reinig from SEO.

Thanks to Mélanie Delannoy and Irina Douziech, from SES (Société Européenne des Satellites).

Thanks to Ben Funck, Paul Konsbruck, Markus Leis, Vincent Weynandt, and Perry Wies from LuxConnect. Thanks to Vittorio Santonocito from LuxProvide.

Thanks to Frank Schmälzle from POLYTEC for providing experimental equipment.

From Radioamateurs du Luxembourg, thanks to Neckel Reuland for the guidance.

Thanks to Daniel Weintraub and the Pauline Oliveros Trust.

Finally, thanks to Ludwig Berger, Gaia Ginevra Giorgi, and Nicola Di Croce for activating the Luxembourg Pavilion, and to Erica Overmeer for welcoming us to Ca'Buccari.

We have been thrilled by the collective intelligence mobilized in making this endeavor possible.
Valentin Bansac, Mike Fritsch, Alice Loumeau

© 2025, authors, editors, and Spector Books, Leipzig
First edition, 2025
Printed in the EU
ISBN: 978-3-95905-893-3